CROWDED AIRWAVES

CROWDED AIRWAVES

Campaign Advertising in Elections

JAMES A. THURBER
CANDICE J. NELSON
DAVID A. DULIO
Editors

BROOKINGS INSTITUTION PRESS
Washington, D.C.

Copyright © 2000
THE BROOKINGS INSTITUTION
1775 Massachusetts Avenue, N.W., Washington, D.C. 20036
www.brookings.edu

Library of Congress Cataloging-in-Publication data

Crowded airwaves : campaign advertising in elections / James A. Thurber, Candice J. Nelson, David A. Dulio, editors
    p.   cm.
Includes bibliographical references and index.
ISBN 0-8157-8456-2 (cloth) — ISBN 0-8157-8455-4 (pbk.)
1. Electioneering—United States. 2. Advertising, Political—United States. I. Thurber, James A., 1943– II. Nelson, Candice J., 1949– III. Dulio, David A.
  JK2281.C76 2000   00-008231
  324.7'3'0973—dc21   CIP

9 8 7 6 5 4 3 2 1

The paper used in this publication meets minimum requirements of the American National Standard for Information Sciences—Permanence of Paper for Printed Library Materials: ANSI Z39.48-1984.

Typeset in Sabon

Composition by Cynthia Stock
Silver Spring, Maryland

Printed by R. R. Donnelley and Sons
Harrisonburg, Virginia

Contents

Acknowledgments

THE EDITORS THANK the Pew Charitable Trusts for its support of the Improving Campaign Conduct grant that funded the research in this volume. Special thanks go to Paul C. Light, formerly with Pew and now head of the Governmental Studies division at Brookings Institution, for his commitment to this book and to the enterprise of improving the way election campaigns are waged. Also thanks to Sean Treglia and Michael Delli Carpini of the Pew Charitable Trusts for their support of our endeavors. Rebecca Rimel, president of the Pew Charitable Trusts, has been a major force in improving campaign conduct, the quality of discourse in our electoral processes, and governance in America. We thank her for her strong support of this project and her continued efforts to make a positive difference in our democracy.

Thank you also to Cornelius M. Kerwin, provost of American University, who has played an important and ongoing role in supporting the activities of the Center for Congressional and Presidential Studies and the Campaign Management Institute. At American University we would also like to thank Walter D. Broadnax, dean of the School of Public Affairs, and Karen O'Connor, chair of the Department of Government. We acknowledge the assistance, comments, and encouragement received from Kim Alfano, David Broder, Anita Dunn, Jennifer Dyjak, Adrianne Hari, Leslie McNaugher, John McPhillips, Sam Popkin, and Claudia Thurber.

At the Brookings Institution Press we would also like to thank Nancy Davidson, Christopher Kelaher, Robert Faherty, and Janet Walker, as well as Elizabeth Reed Forsyth, who edited the manuscript, Sherry Smith, who provided the index, and Carlotta Ribar, who proofread the pages.

CROWDED AIRWAVES

CHAPTER ONE

Introduction

DAVID A. DULIO

CANDICE J. NELSON

JAMES A. THURBER

LAWRENCE, KANSAS, OCTOBER 1998. Dennis Moore (D) had been campaigning for nearly one year in hopes of defeating the incumbent representative of Kansas's third congressional district, Vincent Snowbarger (R). Signs that this would be a close race were apparent as early as September 1997, when a poll showed that Moore, a well-known county district attorney, had greater support in the district than the incumbent.[1] As the campaign progressed, the candidates did not distinguish themselves from one another, and the race stayed tight.

The campaign centered on traditional Democrat versus Republican issues such as social security, taxes, education, and gun control. The dialogue between the candidates got especially nasty over social security and Representative Snowbarger's record of votes and statements on the issue. After a debate near the end of the campaign, during which Snowbarger admitted to considering a plan to phase out social security, the Moore campaign aired a radio spot highlighting the confession.

As election day approached, the air wars escalated to the point where each candidate was spending nearly $100,000 a week on television ads. Representative Snowbarger produced only three campaign ads, all of which attacked his opponent.[2] One of these ads tried to link Dennis Moore to Senator Ted Kennedy and to paint Moore as an extremist. Moore's campaign spots included hard-hitting contrast ads, but they also included light

1. Loomis (1998).
2. Loomis (1998), p. 30.

and humorous ads that turned out to be very attractive to voters of the third district. Moore took the high road by placing no negative attack advertisements on television, although some ads did contrast his views with the incumbent's record.

Moore's campaign team produced one contrast ad to distance him from the snarly ads aired previously. In this television ad, Dennis Moore, a fine musician, is shown playing his guitar while referencing issues important to the district. The spot, titled "Pickin'," concluded with Moore looking into the camera and saying, "I hope come election day, you'll be *pickin'* Dennis Moore for Congress."

The contrast and attack ads likely did their job and told voters where each candidate stood on the issues of social security, education, and gun control. However, when exit poll data were examined, voters in the third district said that what they remembered most about the campaign was Dennis Moore's "Pickin'" spot.

CALIFORNIA'S CENTRAL COAST, SPRING 1998. Lois Capps (D) and Tom Bordonaro (R) had just completed a special election campaign to fill the congressional seat vacated by Capps's late husband, Walter Capps. No candidate in the January election garnered a simple majority of votes, which then required the top two candidates—Capps and Bordonaro—to enter a March runoff election. No other federal elections were being contested at this time, which placed the special runoff election for California's twenty-second district on everyone's radar screen, especially that of special interest groups, which played a key role in it. In the initial special election held in January groups like the Christian Coalition, Americans for Limited Terms, U.S. Term Limits, and Planned Parenthood devoted resources to conveying their message. This influx of special interests paled in comparison to the onslaught of special interest money and television advertisements that appeared during the campaign for the March runoff election. Nearly a dozen special interest groups were on the airwaves attacking both candidates on any number of issues.

The Campaign for Working Families (CWF), headed by Gary Bauer, was one of the most visible of these groups. The CWF attacks on Capps's stances on abortion prompted another abortion group, the National Abortion and Reproductive Rights Action League, to launch its own televised campaign attacking Tom Bordonaro as an "extreme" and "dangerous" candidate. In addition, groups that were involved in the January campaign continued their involvement and even increased their presence in the March race, spending more money and airing more television spots than they had in the first election. In addition, groups like the National Rifle Association and the AFL-CIO (American Federation of Labor and Congress of Industrial Organizations) entered the fray, becoming heavy spenders in the special interest air wars.

With groups like these broadcasting their message over the airwaves with such force, one would imagine that issues like abortion, gun control, and term limits were the most important to the voters of California's central coast. But public opinion polls revealed that they were not.[3] Voters of the twenty-second district cared more about issues such as education, federal disaster support (for damage caused by El Niño), the environment, and fiscal responsibility.[4] The special interest groups that were on the airwaves only served to drown out the candidates' messages that were more in tune with the voters. The candidates went so far as to make "public statements expressing [their] frustration [with] an outsider-imposed agenda."[5]

The presence of the numerous issue advocacy groups cluttered the airwaves, undermining the capacity of the candidates to control their own message to the voters. The interest groups from outside the district changed the strategy, theme, and message of the campaign. According to one observer, this "created an impression that the special election had become a referendum between . . . a dozen Washington-based groups rather than a local determination of congressional succession."[6]

Political advertising plays a key role in modern electioneering and has been part of political campaigns since the earliest federal elections were held in the United States. The experiences of Dennis Moore and Lois Capps with negative and attack advertising and with ads run by special interest groups are typical of the challenges facing candidates in modern American elections. As the modes of mass communication have changed, so have the venues for campaign advertising by candidates, political parties, and interest groups. First newspapers, then radio, and then, in the early 1960s, television entered the process. Early in the next century the Internet likely will be added to the list.

3. Lou Cannon, "Single Issue Ads Driving California Race," *Washington Post,* February 21, 1998, p. A4.

4. Gill (1998).

5. Gill (1998), p. 11.

6. Gill (1998), p. 6.

Not only have the outlets for political advertising expanded over the past twenty years but so have the users of political advertising. Political advertising once was used primarily by candidates; the most recent elections have seen an explosion in the use of advertising not only by candidates but also by political parties and interest groups. As political advertising becomes a more pervasive medium for delivering messages from a variety of sources, understanding the role of political advertising in election campaigns becomes all the more important.

Studies on the Effects of Campaign Communications

Scholars have studied the effects of campaign communications for more than fifty years. After a time prior to 1940 during which the assumption of the "massive propaganda impact [of] the persuasive contents of the mass media" went unchallenged, scholars began to doubt the power of campaign communication.[7] Studies such as *The People's Choice* showed that nearly half of all voters made their electoral choices six months before election day and only a quarter made them during the traditional campaign season (after Labor Day). Theories that campaign communications reinforced, rather than persuaded, the electorate's attitudes began to dominate. Scholars such as Klapper concluded that mass communication was an agent of reinforcement rather than of change.[8]

It was not until the introduction, and subsequent domination, of television that scholars again began to tout the power of paid advertising. Television gradually became a dominant force in American culture. It eventually became the prime source of political and electoral information for many Americans.[9] It is no surprise, therefore, that campaigns began to turn to television as a means for communicating their message. Another development that led to the discovery of the effects of paid political advertising was the waning of citizens' allegiance to political parties.[10] As other scholars have argued, parties became less important and individual candidates became more important in the waging of elections.[11] As candidate-centered elections became a political reality, candidates and their teams of

7. Blumler and Gurevitch (1982), p. 242.
8. Klapper (1960).
9. Blumler and Gurevitch (1982).
10. Wattenberg (1990a).
11. Wattenberg (1990b); Aldrich (1995); Beck and Sorauf (1991); Crotty (1984); Broder (1972).

consultants gravitated toward television as a means for disseminating their message.[12]

The most significant development in the study of political advertising came from within the discipline of political science. Scholars who studied political communication changed their focus from persuasion to cognition research. Most early research focused on how much political communications persuaded the electorate to vote for one candidate or another or to adopt a certain position on an issue.[13] However, more modern research began to focus on individuals' cognition.[14] This shift in focus led the way for work that has identified the power of television advertising to set agendas (see, for example, Herrnson and Patterson in chapter 5 of this volume as well as Iyengar and Kinder 1987) and prime the electorate.[15]

At the very least, campaign advertising conveys information to the electorate. Each chapter in this volume exhibits this and goes beyond. However, there is some debate in the literature over exactly who in the electorate is affected by the information conveyed in political advertisement. Research focusing on the cognitive processing of information is the basis for much of this debate. Zaller's seminal work illustrates the effects of political awareness on the susceptibility of individuals to take in and be affected by political information during campaigns.[16] Ansolabehere and Iyengar show similar differences across individuals' level of partisanship.[17] Other scholars have shown how factors such as prior political knowledge, interest in politics, partisan intensity, and education affect the amount of information that individuals receive and process from campaign messages.[18] In addition, Kahn and Kenney (in chapter 4 of this volume) illustrate that many of these factors are important predictors of the level of information retained by individuals in campaigns.

We know that political advertising conveys information to voters. Less well understood, however, is how information is conveyed through political advertising. This question is addressed by the chapters in this book. In

---

12. Thurber and Nelson (2000).

13. For example, Lazarsfeld, Berelson, and Gaudet (1944); Berelson, Lazarsfeld, and McPhee (1954).

14. Blumler and Gurevitch (1982).

15. Ansolabehere and Iyengar (1995). On the power of television advertising specifically, see Herrnson and Patterson in chapter 5 of this volume, as well as Iyengar and Kinder (1987).

16. Zaller (1992).

17. Ansolabehere and Iyengar (1995).

18. For prior political knowledge, see Converse (1962, 1964); for interest in politics, see Dalager (1996); for partisan intensity, see Miller and Shanks (1996); Ansolabehere and Iyengar (1995); and for education, see Rosenstone and Hansen (1993).

this age of technology and mass communication, paid political advertising is a crucial element of a sophisticated campaign. Candidates deliver their campaign messages to voters using a variety of paid and earned media strategies and tools. Yet the airwaves are being deluged by ads not only from candidates but also from political parties and interest groups. How do these ads affect voters? This book addresses these questions and more. Are some types of ads more successful than others in informing and motivating voters? For example, one controversial issue is the role of "negative" ads in elections. This volume defines and examines negative ads from several perspectives, but that is not the only focus of the research. Also explored is the more general question of the role that ads play in connecting the messages of political actors in the electoral process with the substance and style of the information that voters take with them into the voting booth on election day.

Central Themes of the Book

The chapters in this book focus on three of the most interesting and complicated issues in political advertising today: (1) the characterization of ads and the need to measure the impact of different types of ads, (2) the agenda-setting and priming effects of ads, and (3) the role and consequences of issue advertising for the electorate. The volume begins with an examination of how ads are characterized and, more specifically, with a look at the debate surrounding negative ads. Chapter 2 provides a review of the research on negative advertising. Richard Lau and Lee Sigelman present an extensive summary of the scholarly evidence concerning negative ads in election campaigns. Lau and Sigelman combed through a large number of published and unpublished research devoted to political advertising in an effort to identify studies that assess the effects of negative advertising. After an exhaustive search, they identified forty-one studies. They organize their review of the literature around four assertions that have come to be widely accepted as fact among those who write about negative advertising: (1) negative ads are processed and remembered more readily than positive ads; (2) negative ads work—they improve the evaluations of their sponsor and undermine those of the sponsor's opponent; (3) the electorate dislikes negative ads; and (4) the growth of negative ads has serious and unintended consequences for representative democracy in America.

Another thorny issue in the discussion of negative advertising is what "negative" means in the parlance of political advertising. In chapter 3 Kathleen Hall Jamieson, Paul Waldman, and Susan Sherr address two questions: (1) how should negativity be defined in a political advertisement, and (2) how should the amount of negativity in a political campaign be determined? Their work challenges previously published scholarship and strives to improve our understanding of the components of a political ad. Jamieson and her colleagues argue that to look at political ads as only *positive* or *negative* creates a false dichotomy and ignores *contrast* ads, which include both *attack* and *advocacy*. They suggest that contrast ads give voters reasons to vote *for* as well as against a candidate. By advancing the position that political decisions should be made by weighing both sides of an issue, they argue that contrast ads provide a useful ingredient in campaign discourse. They also suggest new ways of measuring the level of attack advertising in campaigns.

In chapter 4 Kim Fridkin Kahn and Patrick Kenney address another issue surrounding negative advertising—namely, the question of whether there are positive benefits to negative ads. Kahn and Kenney hypothesize that negative ads create a more informed public, because people learn more about candidates and issues from negative ads than from positive ads. They argue, first, that negative information is viewed by citizens as more novel and, therefore, more memorable and, second, that negative ads often provide citizens with details about the potential costs of their decisions and that people are more motivated to avoid costs than to achieve gains in their daily lives. They test their hypotheses by looking at U.S. Senate elections between 1988 and 1992. They use both the National Election Study's Senate Election Study and the Political Commercial Archive at the University of Oklahoma as data sources.

Chapters 5 and 6 turn from the explicit questions surrounding negative advertising to the more general question of the role of campaign advertising in agenda setting and priming in elections. Both Paul Herrnson and Kelly Patterson, in chapter 5, and Shanto Iyengar and John Petrocik, in chapter 6, address the question of whether campaigns matter. Herrnson and Patterson look at U.S. House of Representatives elections in 1992 to assess the impact of candidates' campaign communications and agenda setting. Their study uses a unique data set that enables them to systematically assess the impact of congressional campaign agendas on voting behavior. Using both the Voter Research Surveys and General Election Exit Poll in 1992 and a mail survey sent to 1992 Democrat and Republican candidates and their campaign managers, Herrnson and Patterson identify both the issues that candidates thought were most important in their elections as well as the issues that voters identified as most important in their voting choices.

In chapter 6 Iyengar and Petrocik challenge the literature that argues that methodological difficulties in measuring voters' exposure to campaigns make it difficult to assess the impact of campaigns on elections. Using both experimental and survey research, they examine the effect of campaigns on basic rule voting. The authors investigate whether campaigns matter by testing the effect of "fundamental political conditions"—namely, partisanship and assessments of an incumbent's job performance. They argue that these two components produce a "basic rule" for voters: if partisan, a voter votes his or her party affiliation (also called the "party rule"); if nonpartisan, a voter makes his or her decision based on an evaluation of the incumbent's job performance; if partisan but unwilling to support the party's nominee, a voter also uses the logic of incumbent approval.

Chapter 7 moves from evaluations of advertising in candidate-centered campaigns to an examination of issue advocacy campaigns. Darrell West argues that these campaigns raise a series of problems for election scholars. West addresses the difficulties in disentangling the effect of issue ads from all the other means of communication in an election. He also addresses the normative questions of the consequences of issue ads for representative democracy and evaluates what he sees as the three major options for dealing with the problems raised by issue advocacy in American elections.

In chapter 8 we revisit the findings presented in the preceding chapters and discuss the theoretical, empirical, methodological, normative, and practical contributions they make to our understanding of political advertising. This book by no means exhausts the debate on the role of political advertising—particularly negative political advertising—in election campaigns at the beginning of the twenty-first century. However, we think it does a good job of summarizing much of what scholarship in this area has taught us.

References

Aldrich, John. 1995. *Why Parties? The Origin and Transformation of Political Parties in America.* University of Chicago Press.

Ansolabehere, Stephen, and Shanto Iyengar. 1995. *Going Negative: How Political Advertisements Shrink and Polarize the Electorate.* Free Press.

Beck, Paul Allen, and Frank J. Sorauf. 1991. *Party Politics in America,* 7th ed. Harper-Collins.

Berelson, Bernard, Paul F. Lazarsfeld, and William N. McPhee. 1954. *Voting: A Study of Opinion Formation in a Presidential Campaign.* University of Chicago Press.

Blumler, Jay G., and Michael Gurevitch. 1982. "The Political Effects of Mass Communication." In Michael Gurevitch and others, eds., *Culture, Society, and the Media*. London: Methuen.

Broder, David S. 1972. *The Party's Over: The Failure of Politics in America*. Harper and Row.

Converse, Philip E. 1962. "Information Flow and Stability of Partisan Attitudes." *Public Opinion Quarterly* 26 (winter): 578–99.

———. 1964. "Nature and Belief Systems in Mass Publics." In David Apter, ed., *Ideology and Discontent*. Free Press.

Crotty, William. 1984. *American Political Parties in Decline*, 2d ed. Little, Brown.

Dalager, Jon K. 1996. "Voters, Issues, and Elections: Are the Candidates' Messages Getting Through?" *Journal of Politics* 58 (May): 486–515.

Gill, Jeff. 1998. "One Year and Four Elections: A Case Study of Campaign Conduct in the 1998 Capps Campaign for California's Twenty-Second District." Paper presented at the conference Money, Media, and Madness, American University, Center for Congressional and Presidential Studies, Washington, D.C., December.

Iyengar, Shanto, and Donald R. Kinder. 1987. *News That Matters*. University of Chicago Press.

Klapper, Joseph T. 1960. *The Effects of Mass Communication*. Free Press.

Lazarsfeld, Paul F., Bernard Berelson, and Hazel Gaudet. 1944. *The People's Choice*. Columbia University Press.

Loomis, Burdett A. 1998. "The Kansas 3rd District: 'Pros from Dover' Set up Shop." Paper presented at the conference Money, Media, and Madness, American University, Center for Congressional and Presidential Studies, Washington, D.C., December.

Miller, Warren E., and J. Merrill Shanks. 1996. *The New American Voter*. Harvard University Press.

Rosenstone, Steven J., and John Mark Hansen. 1993. *Mobilization, Participation, and Democracy in America*. Macmillan.

Thurber, James A., and Candice J. Nelson, eds. 2000. *Campaign Warriors: Political Consultants in Elections*. Brookings.

Wattenberg, Martin P. 1990a. *The Decline of American Political Parties: 1952– 1988*. Harvard University Press.

———. 1990b. *The Rise of Candidate-Centered Politics: Presidential Elections of the 1980s*. Harvard University Press.

Zaller, John. 1992. *The Nature and Origins of Mass Opinion*. Cambridge University Press.

CHAPTER TWO

Effectiveness of Negative Political Advertising

RICHARD R. LAU

LEE SIGELMAN

RUNNING FOR POLITICAL OFFICE in the United States has never been recommended for the thin-skinned or faint-hearted. Lord Bryce, visiting these shores in the 1880s, characterized American campaigns as "a tempest of invective and calumny."[1] To judge from the volume of complaints about the negativism of political campaigns, matters have only gotten worse since then. Although negativism in campaigning has fluctuated markedly over the years, it entered its current "up" stage in the late 1970s, when political action committees targeted numerous congressional incumbents for attack.

The 1998 mid-term elections did nothing to reverse this trend. In the weeks leading up to the election, the airwaves were saturated with political advertisements. Approximately 35 percent more political ads were aired in 1998 than in the 1994 mid-term election, and local newscasts in the weeks before the 1998 election contained four times as many ads by the candidates as stories about the campaign.[2] The result was a "carpet-bombing" of the public with a barrage of "fiercely negative" ads.[3] In the year's main event, the New York senatorial contest between incumbent Alfonse D'Amato (R) and Representative Charles Schumer (D), the contenders

1. Bryce (1889).
2. Lisa de Moraes, "The TV Column," *Washington Post*, October 29, 1998, p. D13.
3. Howard Kurtz, "Attack Ads Carpet TV; High Road Swept Away," *Washington Post*, October 20, 1998, pp. A1, A5.

seemed determined to outdo one another in delivering low blows and cheap shots: D'Amato called Schumer, among other things, a "putzhead," and Schumer charged, among other things, that D'Amato was a "bully taking lunch money from hungry kids." The same scenario was played out in hundreds of other races across the nation, although in somewhat less imaginative language. And in Tennessee, the ultimate in attack campaigning occurred when Tommy Burks, a candidate for reelection to the state senate, was shot to death, apparently by his Republican opponent, Byron (Low Tax) Looper, who conducted the last two weeks of his campaign from jail. On November 3, Looper got 3 percent of the votes cast, with his write-in opponent, Charlotte Burks, the widow of the decedent, receiving the remaining 97 percent.

This upsurge in negativism, which continued in 1998 and into the 2000 presidential primary season, often is attributed to the increasing dominance of television in modern political campaigns. In the era before television, when newspapers were openly partisan, the mass media were thought to have minimal political effect, largely reinforcing existing attitudes and commitments.[4] By the early 1960s, however, the vast majority of American homes had television sets, and changing professional norms in the mass media led to more balanced treatment of politics in newspapers and on radio and television. As a consequence, when one encounters an openly partisan message on television these days, one can be reasonably certain that it soon will be counterbalanced by another equally but oppositely partisan message *or* that it is a paid advertisement. The "on-the-one-hand, on-the-other-hand" format that currently defines balance in news coverage evokes little criticism, but the presumed effectiveness of political advertisements is viewed widely as a major problem for American democracy.

When skillfully used, television's multiple modes of communication and powerful ability to orient attention can invite strong, unthinking negative responses in low-involvement viewers. And, by overloading our information-processing capacity with rapidly paced information, televised political ads can short-circuit the normal defenses that more educated, more highly involved viewers ordinarily marshal against suspect claims.[5]

4. See, for example, Berelson, Lazarsfeld, and McPhee (1954); Lazarsfeld, Berelson, and Gaudet (1948).

5. Jamieson (1992), p. 50.

Recognizing the medium's ability to transmit messages rapidly, widely, and dramatically, more and more candidates for high office are building their campaign strategies around television advertising. In the 1996 presidential election campaign, the Clinton and Dole forces poured well over $100 million—more than 60 percent of their combined budgets—into electronic advertising.[6]

What sorts of ads are they getting for their money? Although some candidates engage in only mild forms of "comparative advertising" and others avoid negative appeals altogether, many campaign ads amount to "thirty-second snarls" designed to "criticize, discredit, or belittle their opponents rather than promoting their own ideas and programs."[7] The formula is simple:

> In clipped, agitated tones, attack your opponent's character. Distort his record. Associate her with extremists or unpopular political figures. To awaken fear, work in a between-the-lines racist message; to foster suspicion, insinuate corrupt behavior. And by all means, steer clear of substantive issues.[8]

What are the consequences of all of this negative political advertising? Are attack ads really as potent a political force as they are made out to be? According to both social-psychological and rational choice theories, "going negative" *should* work, and there clearly is no shortage of dramatic examples and expert testimony that it *does* work.[9] Citing instances in which attack ads are thought to have been instrumental in turning a campaign around, such as Mitch McConnell's upset defeat of Walter Huddleston in a 1984 Senate race and George Bush's come-from-behind victory over Michael Dukakis in 1988, campaign strategists portray attack advertising as a potent political force:

> *Richard Wirthlin (Republican pollster):* A negative attack can take a virtual unknown against an apparently strong incumbent and provide a tremendous and strong margin.[10]

6. Ira Chinoy, "In Presidential Race, TV Ads Were Biggest '96 Cost by Far," *Washington Post,* March 31, 1997, p. A19.

7. George F. Will, "Fingernails across the Blackboard," *Newsweek,* October 31, 1994, p. 72; Ansolabehere et al. (1994), p. 829.

8. Reginald K. Brack Jr., "How to Clean up Gutter Politics," *New York Times,* December 27, 1994, p. A21.

9. For social-psychological theory, see Lau (1985); for rational choice theory, see Davis and Ferrantino (1996); Riker (1991, 1997); Skaperdas and Grofman (1996).

10. "Negative Spots Likely to Return in Election '88," *Advertising Age,* September 14, 1987, p. 3.

Jill Buckley (Democratic consultant): People say they hate negative advertising. But it works. They hate it and remember it at the
same time. The problem with positive is that you have to run it again
and again and again to make it stick. With negative, the poll numbers will move in three or four days.[11]

Roger Stone (Republican consultant): Voters will tell you in focus
groups that they don't like negative ads, but they retain the information so much better than the positive ones. The point is: People like
dirty laundry. Why do tabloids sell?[12]

Susan Estrich (manager of the 1988 Dukakis campaign): Candidates engage in negative campaigning because it works. No matter
how much people say they dislike it, negative campaigns continue to
move voters from one column to the other.[13]

Mike Murphy (manager of the 1996 Bob Dole campaign): People
say they don't like negative ads, but negative information is an important part of their decisionmaking. It works. Campaigns are a
"whatever works" kind of world.[14]

Philip Friedman (Democratic consultant): Polls show there's nothing good about politicians that people will believe, and nothing bad
they won't believe. The big question in most campaigns . . . is whose
negative campaign is better. If it's negative, it works. If it's positive,
save it for your tombstone.[15]

Practitioners of attack advertising contend that it works and try to take
advantage of it. Critics of attack advertising readily concede that it works,
although they are unhappy about it. Pundit Charles Krauthammer's perspective is typical:

It is easy to discount advertising on the grounds that no one could be
so stupid as to believe it. . . . Can anyone really believe that beer
makes men attractive to women? Yet that pitch continues to be made,

11. Alan Ehrenhalt, "Technology, Strategy Bring New Campaign Era," *Congressional
Quarterly Weekly Report,* December 7, 1985, p. 2560.

12. Steven W. Colford, "Polls Accentuated Negative," *Advertising Age,* November 10,
1986, p. 104.

13. Susan Estrich, "Mudslinging Is Big Voter Turnoff," *USA Today,* June 10, 1993,
p. 11A.

14. Howard Kurtz, "The GOP's Negative Force: Political Image-Maker Mike Murphy,"
Washington Post, November 1, 1994, p. C1.

15. Melinda Henneberger, "As Political Ads Slither into Negativity, the Real Venom Is
Not Found on TV," *New York Times,* October 30, 1994, p. 45.

year in and year out, for the simple reason that it works. So does negative political advertising.[16]

At the same time that critics concede that attack advertising "works," they decry it as a corrosive influence on participatory democracy, as "the electronic equivalent of the plague."[17] Beset by the unseemly spectacle of candidates doing "whatever it takes" to win (as George Bush vowed in 1992), countless critics, like millions of citizens, are appalled. In the words of Democratic consultant Daniel Payne:

> Challengers are selling anger. . . . And incumbents are selling fear. . . . The airwaves are filled with contentious crap. On Monday, Candidate A calls Candidate B a name. On Tuesday, B says, "I'm not that, and what's more, A is this." Voters are just sickened by the whole thing.[18]

As another political consultant has observed:

> In a campaign of negative ads fighting negative ads, what incentive is there for the viewer to go to the polls? Obviously, both these candidates are turkeys. The potential voter is left with a disgruntled sentiment that it's a shame someone has to win.[19]

In short, attack campaign advertising is widely considered pervasive and problematic, and both its pervasiveness and the problems it poses for participatory democracy are seen as stemming from its effectiveness. If attack advertising were assumed to be ineffective, then untold millions of dollars presumably no longer would be spent on attack ads every election year, and all the hand-wringing about the baleful effects of negative advertising could be relaxed. But is it safe to treat the effectiveness of attack advertising as a given? Perhaps the case is not as clear as it is assumed to be; after all, conventional wisdom does sometimes turn out to be wrong. The more closely one listens to the claims made by both practitioners and critics of attack advertising, the more extravagant those claims begin to sound. For one thing, practitioners and critics alike tend to dwell on instances in which attack advertising is thought to have been decisive, ignor-

16. Charles Krauthammer, "Why Americans Hate Politicians," *Time*, December 9, 1991, p. 92.
17. West (1993), p. 51.
18. Quoted by Robert Guskind, "Airborne Attacks," *National Journal*, October 31, 1992, p. 2479.
19. Quoted by Laczniak and Caywood (1987), p. 21.

ing counterexamples. The failed presidential campaigns of George Bush in 1992 and Bob Dole in 1996 and Michael Huffington's losing Senate bid against Dianne Feinstein in 1994 serve as reminders that attackers do not always win. Nor, for that matter, *can* attackers always win, for in some campaigns both candidates go on the attack—as in the 1996 New Jersey Senate race between Robert Torricelli (D) and Dick Zimmer (R) and in the 1994 Virginia Senate campaign pitting Oliver North (R) against Charles Robb (D).[20]

Rather than continuing to take political practitioners and pundits at their word when they testify to the potency of attack advertising, what we need at this point is a careful sifting of the evidence. In recent years a substantial body of research has accumulated on political advertising in general and attack advertising in particular. In this research literature, the standard indicator of whether an ad is negative is whether it focuses primarily on the sponsor's opponent, in which case it would be classified as an "attack," or not, in which case it would be classified as a positive or "advocacy" ad. It has been argued forcefully that a more refined distinction needs to be made among "advocacy," "attack," and "comparison" or "contrast" ads, where contrast ads refer to ads in which sponsors make claims both in favor of their own candidacy and in criticism of their opponent. Despite these arguments, we continue to employ the traditional positive versus negative dichotomy here (although we try to employ the arguably less loaded terms "advocacy" and "attack"), because our follow-up analyses have indicated that the introduction of a category for "contrast ads" does nothing to alter the findings.[21]

What do these studies, taken as a whole, reveal? Does the preponderance of evidence bear out the claims about attack advertising that have been made so often and are accepted so widely? To answer these questions, we have carefully reviewed both published and unpublished research on political attack advertising. Following a brief discussion of the methods we used to locate research studies, we organize our review around four sets of assertions that have come to be accepted as fact among those who think and write about political advertising. First, attack advertisements are processed and remembered more readily than advocacy advertisements. Second, attack ads usually achieve their intended consequences. That is, they improve evaluations of their sponsor and increase the sponsor's

20. Lau, Pomper, and Mumoli (1998).

21. See Jamieson, Waldman, and Sherr (chapter 3 of this volume) for evidence to the contrary.

election prospects, they undermine evaluations of their target and diminish the target's chances of being elected, or both. Third, viewers dislike political attack ads. And fourth, the growing use of political attack ads has serious unintended consequences for American democracy.

Method

The first step in any literature review is to compile a comprehensive inventory of the research literature. Our starting point was the large number of studies of political advertising we had accumulated over the years, including many unpublished convention papers and manuscripts we had been asked to review. We identified other studies by searching pertinent databases and documents, including *ABC Pol Sci, Communication Abstracts, Current Contents, Dissertation Abstracts, PsycINFO, Psychological Abstracts, Social Sciences Index, United States Political Science Documents,* and the programs for meetings of various professional associations. We also combed through the sources cited in each study we had located to identify additional studies that might contain pertinent findings. Next, we contacted the authors of all the relevant studies we had located, described our project, emphasized the importance of including all studies irrespective of the strength, direction, or statistical significance of the results, and requested any additional papers they might know of or have in their possession. Lastly, we used our initial presentation of findings at the American Political Science Association convention in August 1997 to publicize this project and our need for relevant research studies.[22] Our aim was to identify every relevant study. We undoubtedly have missed some, but we believe we have located the great majority.

One of us screened every paper, article, chapter, or book in the inventory to determine whether it reported findings that constituted *an assessment of the effects of political attack advertising.* Our focus on studies that assessed the effects of attack ads led us to exclude from consideration studies of the effectiveness of political advertising that did not distinguish between advocacy and attack ads, marketing studies of attack advertising that did not explicitly consider politicians as one of the "products" being sold, studies of the impact of scandals on the outcome of congressional elections or of candidate attacks in campaign debates that lacked any advertising component, and studies that did not include a means of gauging

22. Lau and others (1997).

the *effects* of attack advertising—either a "no advertisements" control group or an "advocacy advertisements" comparison group.[23] We also tried to avoid "double counting" data reported in more than one venue. For example, we do not comment on the experimentally based findings of Ansolabehere and others because those findings were based on 1,655 subjects who were a subset of the 2,216 subjects in a more comprehensive presentation that we did include in our review.[24] However, a data set could provide multiple findings for our review if it contained multiple types of outcome measures (for example, subjects' evaluations of both the sponsor and the target of an ad).

Results

In all, we identified fifty-five studies, many of which presented findings relevant to two or more of the four assertions stated above. In the remainder of this chapter we examine the validity of those four assertions, based on evidence presented in the fifty-five studies that contained pertinent findings.

Are Political Attack Ads Processed and Remembered More Readily Than Advocacy Ads?

Attack ads are believed to have such pervasive effects because they are presumed to be noticed, processed, and thus remembered more readily than advocacy ads. Indeed, from the perspective of cognitive psychology, better recall would be taken as evidence of greater salience, deeper processing, or both. Fourteen studies in our review speak to this point, summarized in table 2-1. Five of these studies involve surveys, and the remainder are based on experiments.

We begin with an important methodological caveat. This is a difficult question to answer via survey research unless the researcher has detailed information about how often respondents were exposed to the attack and

---

23. Budesheim, Houston, and DePaola (1996); Karrh and Halpern (1997). For example, we excluded the following: for studies that did not distinguish between advocacy and attack ads, Atkin and Heald (1976); Brians and Wattenberg (1996); for studies that did not consider politicians as products being sold, Putrevu and Lord (1994); for studies that lacked any advertising component, Welch and Hibbing (1997); Roese and Sande (1993); and for studies that did not include a means of gauging the effects of attack advertising, Roese and Sande (1993).

24. Ansolabehere and others (1994); Ansolabehere and Iyengar (1995).

Table 2-1. *Memory of Political Advocacy and Attack Advertisements*

Author	Brief study description	Results
Basil, Schooler, and Reeves (1991)	Experiment with local community residents and subjects who saw two "campaigns" consisting of three advocacy or three attack ads for each candidate in an actual Senate election from another state	Advocacy ads were recalled better than attack ads
Brians and Wattenberg (1996)	Nationally representative survey of respondents recalling any political ad from the 1992 presidential election	Political attack ads were more likely to be recalled than advocacy ads, relative to an estimate of their actual prevalence during the 1992 campaign
Hitchon and Chang (1995)	Experiment with undergraduate subjects manipulating exposure to advocacy, neutral, and attack ads for female and male gubernatorial candidates	Candidates using attack ads were less likely to be recalled than candidates using advocacy ads
Kaid, Chanslor, and Hovind (1992)	Experiment with college student and community resident subjects manipulating exposure to actual advocacy or attack, issue or image televised political ads	Aspects of advocacy issue ads were remembered more frequently than aspects of attack ads
Kaid, Leland, and Whitney (1992)	Experiment with undergraduate subjects manipulating exposure to advocacy and attack ads for Bush and Dukakis	No significant difference in how likely advocacy and attack ads were remembered
King, Henderson, and Chen (1998)	Experiment with undergraduates as subjects manipulating exposure to advocacy/attack ads from Clinton/Dole campaigns, controlling on prior liking of candidates	Advocacy Clinton ads were significantly more likely to be recalled than attack Clinton ads. There were no differences in memory for advocacy or attack Dole ads
Lang (1991)	Experiment with undergraduate subjects manipulating exposure to eight randomly selected advocacy and attack ads varying in emotional appeal and audio-visual format	More information was recalled about attack ads than advocacy ads

Study	Description	Finding
Lemert, Elliot, Berstein, Rosenberg, and Nestvold (1991)	Representative sample of survey respondents reflecting on an advocacy or attack ad they recalled seeing during 1988 presidential election	Attack ads were much more likely to be recalled
Merritt (1984)	Representative survey of respondents in a local area, reflecting on their exposure to attack and neutral ads for candidates in a state assembly race	Attack ad was more likely to be correctly recalled
Newhagen and Reeves (1991)	Experiment with local residents as subjects, reacting to actual Bush and Dukakis advocacy, attack, or comparative ads from the 1988 presidential election	Recall was more accurate (and quicker) for attack than advocacy ads
Roberts (1995)	Nationally representative telephone survey of respondents after the 1992 presidential election, asked to recall Bush or Clinton ads	No significant difference in recall of advocacy or attack Bush or Clinton ads
Shapiro and Rieger (1992)	Experiment with undergraduate subjects manipulating exposure to advocacy or attack issue or image radio ads for two fictitious candidates in two local elections	Attack ads were more likely to be remembered
Sulfaro (1998)	Reported memory (on NES surveys) for advocacy or attack ad from the 1992 and 1996 U.S. presidential elections	An attack ad was more likely to be recalled than an advocacy ad, irrespective of years of education
Thorson, Christ, and Caywood (1991)	Experiment with undergraduate subjects manipulating exposure to fictitious issue or image support or attack ads created for actual Senate candidates	Memory was better for advocacy rather than attack ad

advocacy ads they were trying to recall.[25] For example, survey respondents may be more likely to remember seeing negative than advocacy ads, but if they also were *exposed* to many more negative ads, this would not constitute greater recall. The five survey-based findings included in table 2-1 are pertinent only because respondents during those elections appear to have been exposed to approximately equal numbers of attack and advocacy advertisements; more precisely, approximately equal numbers of attack and advocacy ads were run in the media markets in which these respondents lived, from which it is not too great an inferential leap to conclude that they were exposed to approximately equal numbers of ads of each type. Four of the five survey-based studies found that, as expected, negative ads are more memorable.

But surveys are clearly second-best evidence on this point. Experiments are much more powerful designs for testing recall, because it is so much easier to control exposure to the different ads being recalled. A recent example of such research is provided by Hitchon and Chang, who were interested in the effects of gender on voters' perceptions of female and male candidates.[26] Experimental subjects were exposed to eleven television advertisements, five "filler" ads to help disguise the purpose of the study, and six ads from three gubernatorial elections in which a woman was running against a man. All six candidates (each of whom was running for governor of another state, so that it could be assumed that the experimental subjects had never seen any of the ads before) had produced advocacy, attack, and neutral ads. This enabled the researchers to create a randomized experiment in which subjects were exposed to all combinations of advocacy, attack, and neutral ads from both male and female candidates but were exposed to only one ad from any particular candidate. After viewing the ads, the subjects were asked to provide specific information about each one (such as a candidate's name). Contrary to the conventional wisdom, information about candidates using advocacy ads was more likely to be recalled than information about candidates using attack ads.

Nor was the Hitchon and Chang study an exception. Of the fourteen studies with pertinent findings, seven found superior information recall in attack advertisements, but five found exactly the opposite (that is, better recall of advocacy than attack ads), and two reported no differences in

25. For example, Goldstein (1997).
26. Hitchon and Chang (1995).

recall based on the negativism of the ads. Particularly given that more than half of the positive results (for example, attack ads are better remembered) come from surveys where we cannot be sure about the actual exposure to the different types of ads, we do not consider it prudent to answer this question in the affirmative. At the very least, there is no strong preponderance of evidence indicating that political attack ads are more memorable than advocacy ads.

Are Political Attack Ads Effective in Achieving Their Intended Consequences?

Do political attack ads improve the evaluations of their sponsors and increase their probability of getting elected, or do they decrease the evaluations of their sponsors' targets (opponents) and diminish their chances of being elected? Because winning elections is the main reason why political advertisements are produced in the first place, it comes as no surprise that this question has drawn the most research. We located thirty-five studies that reported seventy findings that speak to this question, summarized in table 2-2. Some of these findings involved an actual or simulated vote choice between candidates; others focused on evaluations of the sponsor or target of the attack advertisements, where higher evaluations of the sponsor or lower evaluations of the target presumably map onto vote choice. One of the best examples of this type of research is a series of experiments devised by Ansolabehere and Iyengar, who recruited a diverse sample of Los Angeles residents to participate in a study of "selective perception of local news programs."[27] These experimental subjects watched a fifteen-minute local news program into which Ansolabehere and Iyengar had inserted, during one of the regular commercial breaks, a campaign ad for one of the candidates in a statewide race that was then under way in California. There were two versions of each advertisement for each candidate: one presenting the candidate's own program on a particular topic (for example, the environment), the other attacking the opponent's record on the same issue. Although the audio components of the ads varied, the video components were identical and usually came from actual ads produced for the campaign; the only difference between the two was the message conveyed in the announcer's voice-over.

Subjects watched the news program while sitting on a sofa or a comfortable chair in a group of two or three viewers in a small room, much as

27. Ansolabehere and Iyengar (1995), p. 29.

Table 2-2. *Intended Consequences of Political Attack Advertisements*

Author	Brief study description	Results
Ansolabehere and Iyengar (1995)	Experiment manipulating exposure to fictitious advocacy or attack ads for actual candidates inserted into regular commercial break of local news program	Attack ads slightly increased vote intention for their sponsor during general elections, but slightly decreased intended vote for their sponsor during primary elections
Basil, Schooler, and Reeves (1991)	Experiment with local community residents as subjects who saw two "campaigns" consisting of three advocacy or three attack ads from each candidate in an actual Senate election from another state	Sponsoring candidates were liked no better and perceived as no stronger when they presented advocacy or attack ads, but the target was liked significantly less when the sponsor attacked with a negative ad compared to using an advocacy ad about himself
Bullock (1994)	Experiment with randomly selected prospective jurors awaiting assignment as subjects, manipulating exposure to more or less ambiguous issue or image ads for two hypothetical state senate candidates	Both the sponsoring candidate and the opposing candidate were liked less if the sponsor used attack ads rather than advocacy ads; however attack ads caused the likelihood of voting for the targeted candidate to drop significantly
Capella and Taylor (1992)	Authors' judgment of which candidate initiated use of attack ads in 25 1986 Senate campaigns with substantial amounts of attack advertising	Initiator of attack ads lost 18 of 25 elections, a result not significantly different from chance
Garramone, Atkin, Pinkleton, and Cole (1990)	Experiment with undergraduates as subjects manipulating exposure to various combinations and numbers of positive and negative biographical profiles and political commercials for two fictional U.S. Senate candidates	Attack ads caused greater "image discrimination" compared to advocacy ads
Haddock and Zanna (1997)	"Natural" experiment with undergraduates as subjects, examining impressions of actual candidates before and after controversial attack ads aired during 1993 Canadian national election	Affect toward the sponsor of the attack ads decreased slightly after airing of ads, while affect toward the target of the attacks increased slightly after their airing

Study		
Hill (1989)	Experiment with undergraduates as subjects using advocacy or attack ads from Bush or Dukakis campaigns as stimuli	No significant differences in how much the sponsor of attack vs. advocacy ads was liked, but the opponent was liked more if the sponsor used an attack rather than advocacy ad
Hitchon and Chang (1995)	Experiment with undergraduates as subjects manipulating exposure to advocacy, neutral, and attack ads from female and male gubernatorial candidates	Candidates who attacked their opponents were liked less than candidates who used advocacy ads
Hitchon, Chang, and Harris (1997)	Similar experiment with college student subjects manipulating exposure to advocacy, neutral, and attack ads from female and male gubernatorial candidates	Candidates who used attack ads were liked less than candidates who used advocacy or neutral ads
Houston, Doan, and Roskos-Ewolsen (1999)	Two experiments with college student subjects manipulating exposure to three written advocacy or attack "ads" from mock liberal or conservative senate candidates	Sponsors of ads were liked better when their own ads were advocacy; targets of attack ads were generally liked less; however differential liking for the candidate with the same ideology as the subject was greatest when that candidate ran an advocacy campaign and the opponent ran an attack campaign
Kahn and Geer (1994)	Experiment with undergraduates as subjects manipulating exposure to advocacy or attack ads from out-of-state gubernatorial candidates inserted in regular ad breaks during a TV sitcom	Sponsoring candidate was liked slightly less if he used attack compared to advocacy ads, and liked significantly less if subjects were exposed to two attack ads sponsored by that candidate (compared to only one)
Kaid (1997)	Experiment with undergraduates as subjects manipulating exposure to actual ads from the 1996 Clinton or Dole campaigns	A candidate was liked slightly more and his opponent significantly less if subjects were shown an attack rather than advocacy ad produced by that candidate; moreover, subjects were much more likely to say they intended to vote for a candidate after viewing one of his attack ads compared to one advocacy ad

(Table continues on the following page.)

Table 2-2 (continued)

Author	Brief study description	Results
Kaid and Boydston (1987)	Experiment with community residents as subjects, who rated a Congressional candidate from another district before and after seeing one of his actual advocacy or attack ads	Affect for target of ads dropped significantly after viewing the candidate's attack ad, relative to an advocacy ad
Kaid, Chanslor, and Hovind (1992)	Experiment with college student and community resident subjects manipulating exposure to actual advocacy or attack, issue or image televised political ads	Candidates who use attack issue ads were liked much less than candidates who used advocacy issue ads
King and Henderson (1999)	Experiment with undergraduates as subjects manipulating exposure to advocacy/attack ads from Michigan gubernatorial election, controlling on prior liking of candidates	No effect of ad tone on liking for the sponsor or the target of the ad, nor on vote intention. There were some interactions between ad tone and initial attitude toward the candidates, however
King, Henderson, and Chen (1998)	Experiment with undergraduates as subjects manipulating exposure to advocacy/attack ads from Clinton/Dole campaigns, controlling on prior liking of candidates	Both Clinton (the sponsor) and Dole (the target) were liked less when subjects exposed to an attack (rather than advocacy) ad from Clinton; intention to vote for Clinton dropped after exposure to one of his attack ads. There were no effects of exposure to advocacy or attack ads from Dole
Lau, Pomper, and Mumoli (1998)	Nationally representative survey respondents evaluating the major-party candidates from the 1988 and 1990 U.S. Senate elections, who had engaged in varying amounts of attack campaigning, as coded from newspaper accounts; combined with aggregate (state-level) analysis of results of 1988, 1990, 1994, and 1996 Senate elections	There was a negative relationship between relatively greater use of attack campaigning by one of the candidates and vote choice at the individual level, and an almost significant negative relationship ($p < .06$) at the aggregate level
Lemert, Elliot, Berstein, Rosenberg, and Nestvold (1991)	Representative sample of survey respondents reflecting on an advocacy or attack ad they could recall seeing during 1988 presidential election	Sponsor of ad was liked slightly less, and target of the ad was liked much more, if an attack ad (compared to an advocacy ad) was recalled

Study	Method	Findings
Lemert, Wanta, and Lee (1999)	Actual voting in mail-only special senate election in Oregon, by a small random sample of registered voters in the Eugene area (who had voted in prior three senate elections), who did or did not remember a pledge by one of the candidates to stop his attack ads	Respondents of all party affiliations who believed the Democrat lived up to his pledge to stop his attack campaigning were more likely to vote for him, compared to respondents who did not feel the Democrat had lived up to his pledge
Martinez and Delegal (1990)	Experiment with undergraduates as subjects manipulating exposure to attack ads from one or both candidates in a hypothetical election	The more a candidate's campaign was perceived as attack, the less the sponsor was liked and the more the target was liked
Mathews and Dietz-Uhler (1998)	Experiment with undergraduates as subjects manipulating exposure to advocacy or attack "family values" ad from mock Democratic or Republican senate candidate	Subjects were more likely to like and intend to vote for a candidate who sponsored an advocacy ad rather than an attack ad
Merritt (1984)	Representative survey of respondents in a local area, reflecting on their exposure to attack and neutral ads from candidates for a state assembly race	There was significantly more negative affect toward both the opponent and the sponsor when the sponsor's attack rather than advocacy ads were seen
Pfau, Kenski, Nitz, and Sorenson (1989)	Representative sample of 374 likely voters, reporting exposure to attack ad from least preferred candidate during 1988 presidential campaign	Evaluations of the least-preferred candidate were significantly higher, and intentions to vote for him were significantly greater, if respondents reported seeing an attack ad sponsored by the candidate
Pinkleton (1997)	Experiment with undergraduates as subjects manipulating amount of negative information about opponent included in an ad from fictitious candidate	The more negative an ad, the less the target and the sponsor of the ad were liked
Pinkleton (1998)	Experiment with undergraduates as subjects manipulating amount of negative information about opponent included in an ad from fictitious candidate	Both sponsor and target of ads liked somewhat less if ad is attack rather than advocacy

(Table continues on the following page.)

Table 2-2 (*continued*)

Author	Brief study description	Results
Roddy and Garramone (1988)	Experiment with fictitious candidates and undergraduates as subjects manipulating exposure to advocacy or attack response to opponent's issue or image attack ad	After an opponent's attack, there were no significant differences in liking for the sponsor or target of the attack (nor was there any difference in intentions to vote for either candidate) as a function of the advocacy or attack nature of the response
Schultz and Pancer (1997)	Experiment with undergraduates as subjects, manipulating sex of fictitious candidate and whether s/he attacks opponent's character	There were no significant differences in evaluations of the sponsor, nor intentions to vote for him/her, caused by exposure to an attack ad used by that candidate
Shapiro and Rieger (1992)	Experiment with undergraduates as subjects manipulating exposure to advocacy or attack issue or image radio ads from two fictitious candidates in two local elections	Target of an attack ad was liked less than the target of an advocacy ad; but the sponsor of attack ads was liked less than sponsor of advocacy ads, and subjects were much more likely to intend to vote for the sponsor of an advocacy ad rather than an attack ad
Sulfaro (1998)	Reported memory (on ANES surveys) for advocacy or attack ad from the 1992 and 1996 U.S. presidential elections	Sponsor of attack ad liked less, but only by respondents with low education levels. Target of attack ad liked slightly more by respondents of all education levels

Thorson, Christ, and Caywood (1991)	Experiment with undergraduates as subjects manipulating exposure to fictitious issue or image support or attack ads created for actual Senate candidates	Sponsor of an attack ad was liked less than the sponsor of an advocacy ad, and there were no differences in intention to vote for the sponsor caused by the nature of the candidate's ads
Tinkham and Weaver-Lariscy (1991)	Survey of major party candidates in competitive 1982 congressional races, reporting on their media strategy (advocacy issue, advocacy image, or focus on opponent)	Challengers who went negative were more likely to win; but incumbents who went negative were more likely to lose, and candidates in open seats who went negative were much more likely to lose
Tinkham and Weaver-Lariscy (1993)	Experiment with undergraduates as subjects, manipulating exposure to actual political advocacy or attack ads	Sponsor of attack ads liked relatively much less than sponsor of advocacy ads
Wadworth, Patterson, Kaid, Cullers, Malcomb, and Lamirand (1987)	Experiment with undergraduates as subjects, manipulating exposure to advocacy or attack ads from fictitious candidates	No significant difference in liking for the sponsor of advocacy/attack ads
Weaver-Lariscy and Tinkham (1996)	Survey of major party candidates in competitive 1990 congressional races, reporting on their media strategy (advocacy issue, advocacy image, or focus on opponent)	Controlling for incumbency, there was no relationship between campaign strategy and the outcome of the election
Weigold (1992)	Experiment with undergraduates as subjects, manipulating exposure to advocacy or attack ad by fictitious congressional candidate	Both the sponsor and the target of attack ads were liked less than if the sponsor used advocacy ads

they might watch television in their own living room. The thirty-second stimulus ad was only one of six such ads that were shown during the half-hour program. This experiment, in our judgment, may be the very best in the entire field of media research, in that it combines all of the advantages of a carefully controlled laboratory experiment without any real loss of realism. Subjects were asked to do what they normally do anyway: watch television in a familiar setting. Because the experiments were conducted during actual election campaigns, it did not seem at all unusual to see an advertisement for a major candidate during a fifteen-minute news show. This design cleverly masked the real purpose of the experiment, thus avoiding the "demand" characteristics often felt by subjects in experiments. As a consequence, its results are easily generalized to real-world settings.

After viewing the fifteen-minute program, subjects were asked a number of questions about politics and local and national affairs, including whether they intended to vote in the upcoming election and, if so, which candidate they preferred. The results were mixed for vote choice. For experiments conducted during primary elections, attack advertisements appeared to be counterproductive: after viewing a news program into which an attack ad had been inserted, subjects were less inclined to vote for the sponsor of the ad than after viewing a news program into which an advocacy ad had been inserted. Experiments conducted during general election campaigns came to the opposite conclusion: attack ads were somewhat more effective than their advocacy counterparts. Neither of these effects was statistically significant, but both were close.

The mixed results of the Ansolabehere and Iyengar experiments are fairly representative of the findings of this group of studies as a whole. In nineteen of the seventy relevant findings, attack ads were significantly more effective (or nearly so) than comparable advocacy ads; in thirty-three, advocacy ads were significantly more effective than comparable negative ads (or nearly so); and in eighteen, no clear difference emerged between the effectiveness of attack and advocacy ads. In light of the known bias toward publishing statistically significant results, we suspect that if any unpublished findings have escaped our notice, they fall disproportionately into the "no difference" category. Fifty-six of the seventy findings come from experiments, and fourteen are from surveys or related designs, but no differences in the general pattern of results can be attributed to design. Of the fourteen survey-based findings, attack ads were less effective than advocacy ads in eight, attack ads were more effective than advocacy ads in three, and there was no difference between attack and advocacy ads in three. Given the large number of findings reviewed and the large number of settings and subject populations studied, the lack of consensus evidenced in these findings suggests that there is no reason to believe that attack ads are any more likely than advocacy ads to produce the results their sponsors desire—if anything, the opposite is more likely to be true.

Do Viewers Really Dislike Political Attack Ads?

If there is one point on which virtually everyone seems to agree, it is that no one likes political attack ads. Even the proponents of attack advertising concede that these ads are roundly despised. But is this really true? In light of the poor showing of the conventional wisdom in answering our first two questions, we should not take the answer to this question for granted.

Table 2-3 summarizes the findings of the ten studies in our review that report relevant data. One of the best of these studies is that of Tinkham and Weaver-Lariscy, whose subjects evaluated ten commercials, each categorized as either positive or negative, that Washington, D.C.–based political consultants had designated as among their best work.[28] To rule out prior exposure to these ads and existing opinions about the candidates portrayed therein, none of these ads involved nationally visible politicians. After viewing each ad, subjects rated it on fifteen semantic differential dimensions and assigned an overall favorability rating. The least liked of these ads turned out to be an attack advertisement for Mitch McConnell; the most liked was an advocacy advertisement for Buddy Roemer. Overall, the attack ads were rated as significantly less ethical than the advocacy ads.

The findings of this study are reasonably representative of those reported in the other studies in this group. In seven of the ten studies, political attack ads were rated as less ethical, less fair, and otherwise less liked than advocacy ads, while two studies came to the opposite conclusion, and one uncovered no significant differences. Most of the differences, even when statistically significant, are not particularly large, however. (In fairness we should note that our data do not speak directly to the question of whether political attack advertisements are actually "disliked," because the data were not coded against some absolute neutral point. Rather, the comparison is between viewers' liking of attack ads versus their liking of advocacy ads. It may be that one reason the

28. Tinkham and Weaver-Lariscy (1994).

Table 2-3. *Evaluations of Political Advocacy and Attack Advertisements*

Author	Brief study description	Results
Hill (1989)	Experiment with undergraduates as subjects using advocacy or attack ads from Bush or Dukakis campaigns as stimuli	Attack ads were liked more than advocacy ads
Hitchon and Chang (1995)	Experiment with undergraduates as subjects manipulating exposure to advocacy, neutral, and attack ads from female and male gubernatorial candidates	Attack ads produced more negative thoughts than advocacy or neutral ads
King, Henderson, and Chen (1998)	Experiment with undergraduates as subjects manipulating exposure to advocacy/attack ads from Clinton/Dole campaigns, controlling on prior liking of candidates	Exposure to advocacy ads was associated with more positive and fewer negative emotions, compared to exposure to attack ads, in 15/18 comparisons
Pinkleton (1997)	Experiment with undergraduates as subjects manipulating amount of negative information about opponent included in an ad from fictitious candidate	The more negative information there was in an ad, the less it was liked
Pinkleton and Garramone (1992)	Telephone survey of likely voters just before 1990 Michigan statewide election asked respondents to recall and evaluate ads from major senatorial and gubernatorial candidates	There were no significant differences between advocacy and attack ads in how strongly they were approved and in how informative they were judged to be

Roddy and Garramone (1988)	Experiment with fictitious candidates and undergraduates as subjects manipulating exposure to advocacy or attack response to opponent's issue or image attack ad	Attack response ad was liked less than advocacy response ad
Shapiro and Rieger (1992)	Experiment with undergraduates as subjects manipulating exposure to advocacy or attack issue or image radio ads from two fictitious candidates in two local elections	Attack ads were seen as much less fair than advocacy ads
Thorson, Christ, and Caywood (1991)	Experiment with undergraduates as subjects manipulating exposure to fictitious issue or image support or attack ads created for actual Senate candidates	Attack ad was liked less than support ad
Tinkham and Weaver-Lariscy (1994)	Experiment with undergraduates as subjects, all exposed to ten actual political advocacy or attack ads	Attack ads were rated as less ethical than advocacy ads
Wadworth, Patterson, Kaid, Cullers, Malcomb, and Lamirand (1987)	Experiment with undergraduates as subjects manipulating exposure to advocacy or attack ads from fictitious candidates	Attack ad was liked more than advocacy ad

findings in this section are not stronger is that people simply do not like political ads, irrespective of whether the ads exaggerate the good qualities of the sponsor or sling mud at the opponent.) So here, at least, conventional wisdom appears to be on the right side of the issue, although the evidence is by no means uncontested.

Does the Growing Use of Political Attack Ads Have Serious Unintended Consequences for the American System of Government?

The unintended consequence most often attributed to the growth of political attack advertising is a decline in voter turnout, although allegations of this sort also focus on declines in political efficacy and trust in government and a broader darkening of the "public mood." Table 2-4 summarizes thirty-eight findings from twenty-two studies that speak to this point. Of these, the best known are from the Ansolabehere-Iyengar experiments described above. According to these experiments, subjects exposed to a single attack ad by any candidate were about five percentage points less likely to say they were going to vote in the upcoming election than subjects exposed to a single advocacy ad. Ansolabehere and Iyengar went on to examine actual voter turnout rates in races for thirty-four Senate seats in 1992, coding the campaign in each state as primarily positive in tone, primarily negative, or primarily neutral.[29] After controlling for the effects of several other influences on turnout, they found turnout to be about four percentage points lower in states where the "tone" of the campaign was primarily negative than in states where the tone was primarily positive—almost exactly replicating their experimental results.

Looking at these findings as a group, our answer to the fourth question is a very cautious "perhaps." Of the thirty-eight relevant findings, sixteen reported no significant differences, and nine associated *positive* outcomes with attack ads (for example, higher turnout), but thirteen reported significant negative consequences. This pattern of results is not strong enough, in our judgment, to serve as an empirical basis for urging policymakers to begin regulating the content of political ads, but it *is* strong enough to heighten the interest of scholars and others concerned about the American political scene. Concerns about these possible effects should be treated as genuine, but the jury definitely is still out.

29. Ansolabehere and others (1994).

Table 2-4. *Unintentional Consequences of Political Attack Advertisements*

Author	Brief study description	Results
Ansolabehere and Iyengar (1995)	Experiment manipulating exposure to fictitious advocacy or attack ads for actual candidates inserted into regular commercial break of local news program	Attack ads depressed intended turnout for upcoming election; they also decreased political efficacy
Ansolabehere, Iyengar, Simon, and Valentino (1994)	Positive/negative "tone" of thirty-four Senate election campaigns in 1992, coded from newspaper accounts	States with more negative Senate election campaigns had lower turnout
Babbitt and Lau (1994)	Survey data from 1988 and 1990 NES Senate election study, combined with analysis of positive/negative "tone" of the campaigns, coded from newspaper accounts	Issue-based negative campaigning associated with more issue-based knowledge of the challenger but not the incumbent
Brians and Wattenberg (1996)	Nationally representative survey of respondents recalling exposure to political advocacy or attack ad from the 1992 presidential election	Respondents recalling an attack ad were more likely to have voted in the presidential election.
Finkel and Geer (1998)	Examination of aggregate turnout levels in nine presidential elections (1960–92), and reported turnout by survey respondents from those same election years, which differ in the proportion of negative themes in televised ads used by the two major-party presidential candidates	No significant relationship, at either the aggregate or individual level, between relative proportion of negative themes in a candidate's political ads, and turnout
Freedman and Goldstein (1999)	Panel survey of 1997 Virginia gubernatorial election, combined with very sophisticated measure of exposure to advocacy and attack ads from the campaign	Exposure to more attack ads associated with higher turnout but slightly lower political efficacy
Garramone, Atkin, Pinkleton, and Cole (1990)	Experiment with undergraduates as subjects manipulating exposure to various combinations and numbers of positive and negative biographical profiles and political commercials for two fictional U.S. Senate candidates	Attack ads did not significantly affect "likelihood of voting" in election
Geer and Lau (1998)	Aggregate (state-level) turnout and NES survey data from 1960–96 U.S. presidential elections, combined with simulation of possible range of advocacy/attack ads that could have been aired in each state	Particularly at the aggregate level, exposure to more attack ads was associated with higher turnout rates, controlling on many variables often associated with turnout

(Table continues on the following page.)

Table 2-4 *(continued)*

Author	Brief study description	Results
Goldstein (1997)	Aggregate analysis of 1588 counties, and individual-level analysis of survey respondents living in 75 largest media markets, which differed in the actual number of attack ads shown in those media markets by the major presidential candidates during 1996 presidential campaign	The more attack ads run in a county, the lower the aggregate turnout level; however, there was no significant relationship at the individual level between the number of attack ads a survey respondent was exposed to and their probability of voting, or their political efficacy
Houston, Doan, and Roskos-Ewolsen (1999)	Two experiments with college student subjects manipulating exposure to three written advocacy or attack "ads" from mock liberal or conservative senate candidates	No differences in reported likelihood of voting under favorable conditions, but subjects exposed to attack campaigns were less likely to say they would vote under unfavorable conditions
Kahn and Kenny (1999)	Survey data from NES 1988–92 senate election study, combined with coding of sample of ads from those campaigns	Relatively greater use of attack ads associated with slightly higher turnout
Kahn and Kenny (chapter 4 of this volume)	Survey data from NES 1988–92 senate election study, combined with coding of sample of ads from those campaigns	Respondents had greater awareness of major party candidates when relatively more attack ads were produced by candidates
Kaid, Chanslor, and Hovind (1992)	Experiment with college student and community resident subjects manipulating exposure to actual advocacy or attack, issue or image televised political ads	Exposure to advocacy image ads associated with higher levels of intended turnout compared to exposure to attack image ads
Lau, Pomper, and Mumoli (1998)	Aggregate analysis of turnout from the 1988, 1990, 1994, and 1996 U.S. Senate elections, for which the relative positive/negative "tone" of the campaigns had been coded from newspaper accounts	The greater the proportion of attack campaigning by both candidates, the higher the turnout
Lemert, Wanta, and Lee (1999)	Actual voting in mail-only special senate election in Oregon, by a small random sample of registered voters in the Eugene area (who had voted in prior three senate elections), who did or did not remember a pledge by one of the candidates to stop his attack ads	Republicans who recalled an attack ad by the Republican candidate were less likely to vote than Republicans exposed to an advocacy ad by their candidate, but there were no effects on Democrats recalling a Republican ad, nor by either partisan group recalling any of the Democrat's ads

Study	Method	Findings
Luskin and Bratcher (1994)	Aggregate analysis of vote totals from 1986–92 U.S. senate election campaigns, combined with a rating of the negativism of the campaigns, based on newspaper accounts	Campaign negativism decreased turnout in states with higher proportion of independent voters, but otherwise increased turnout
Martinez and Delegal (1990)	Experiment with undergraduates as subjects manipulating exposure to attack ads from one or both candidates in a hypothetical election	No significant relationship between exposure to attack ads and trust in government
McBride, Toburen, and Thomas (1993)	Experiments with undergraduates as subjects manipulating exposure to real political advocacy or attack advertisements	Ad valence did not significantly affect intention to vote in upcoming election, nor actual vote turnout of subjects who could be re-contacted after the election
Pinkleton and Garramone (1992)	Telephone survey of likely voters just before 1990 Michigan statewide election asked respondents to recall and evaluate ads from major senatorial and gubernatorial candidates	No significant relationship between intention to vote and exposure to attack ads
Rahn and Hirshorn (1999)	Experiment with convenience sample of eight-to-thirteen-year-old children manipulating exposure to four advocacy or four attack ads from the 1988 presidential election	Various measures of "public mood" were much lower for children exposed to attack ads
Thorson, Ognianova, Coyle, and Denton (1996)	Representative survey of residents of a northern city after gubernatorial and senatorial election, reporting exposure to advocacy and attack ads from those elections	No significant relationship between relative exposure to advocacy and attack ads and reported turnout, but greater exposure to attack ads was related to lower levels of public mood, lower political efficacy, and slightly lower trust in government
Wattenberg and Brians (1999)	Nationally representative survey of respondents recalling any political ad from the 1992 presidential election	Memory for attack ad associated with slightly higher levels of reported turnout

Conclusions

A quarter of a century ago, McCombs and Shaw attributed the prevailing lack of understanding of the impact of political advertising to the dearth of research on the subject.[30] Since then, a great deal of research has been conducted, but if the research findings surveyed here are to be believed, widespread misunderstandings remain in the form of overly expansive claims about the effects of political attack advertisements. Our review of findings reported in the research literature concludes that attack ads probably are liked less than advocacy ads, but they are not necessarily any more memorable, and there is no good evidence that they are any more effective than advocacy ads in producing the consequences their sponsors intend. However, there is a reasonable chance that, at least in some circumstances, the widespread use of political attack advertisements has consequences that most of us would consider unhealthy for democracy, although such effects are likely to be of very small magnitude.

Of these conclusions, the most surprising—but the one in which we have the greatest confidence, based on existing research—is that political attack ads are no more effective than advocacy ads. Indeed, it would seem that, in accordance with Isaac Newton's third law, for every research finding about the greater effectiveness of attack advertising, there is an equal and opposite research finding about the greater effectiveness of advocacy advertising. This conclusion forces us to confront one final question: *Why is the conventional wisdom about the effectiveness of attack ads so divorced from the evidence provided in the literature?*

There are several possibilities. The first is that the findings cited here are correct but the practitioners who make the advertisements and the pundits who comment on them somehow have been misled into believing that attack ads are more effective than advocacy ads. Part of the answer undoubtedly is that, at least until the splash made by Ansolabehere and Iyengar's *Going Negative*, academic research findings had not even dented the consciousness of those shaping the public discourse about political advertising.[31] This volume may help to change that. Nor are campaigners, consultants, and pundits more immune than the general public and academicians to a wide array of perceptual and attributional biases.[32] In cam-

30. McCombs and Shaw (1972).
31. Ansolabehere and Iyengar (1995).
32. See, for example, Kahneman, Slovic, and Tversky (1982); Fiske and Taylor (1991).

paigns where both sides go on the attack, the well-known tendency toward internal attributions for success and external attributions for failure could lead winners to credit their own "brilliant campaign strategy" and losers to blame their opponent's "vicious attacks." Both of these claims would bolster the impression that attack advertising "works," even though it obviously did not work for the losers.

A different bias that would produce the same result would be the tendency to over-generalize from a vivid example that is easily retrieved from memory. For instance, a reasonably well-informed American, if asked to single out a presidential campaign in which attack advertising was especially prominent, probably would mention 1988, the year of the "Willie Horton" ad. Of course, in the two presidential campaigns since then, the main attacker (Bush in 1992, Dole in 1996) lost, but it is the vivid exception—1988, when Bush's attack ads "worked"—that probably would spring to mind, forging an illusory correlation between attacking and winning. More broadly, people often misperceive, reinterpret, or ignore information that is inconsistent with their preconceptions, and any or all of these tendencies could lead candidates, their advisers, journalists, and political reformers to exaggerate the effectiveness of political attack advertising.

A second possibility is that political attack ads really *are* unusually effective *in practice* but that social science researchers, in creating their experiments, somehow have overlooked the crucial factors that make attack ads effective. No one is claiming that attack ads are more effective in all situations, after all, and perhaps campaign professionals know those situations—know when to use attack advertisements to maximum effect and when not to—but have kept that knowledge to themselves for obvious reasons. If this is so, then, speaking for our fellow academicians, we profess ourselves ready to be enlightened. Again, this volume could prove to be a step in the right direction; and one suggestion, drawn from chapter 6 of this volume, by Iyengar and Petrocik, is that campaigns must be studied much earlier than they typically have been if we are to observe "campaign effects" of any type.

However, even though we are willing to be persuaded, this will not be as easy as one might expect. The findings summarized here are drawn from a meta-analysis of the research literature—a quantitative assessment of the magnitude of effects we have summarized with a broad brush here but have presented in detail elsewhere.[33] In that meta-analysis, we formu-

33. Lau and others (1999).

lated and tested nine hypotheses about situations in which political attack ads might have an advantage over advocacy ads. Not a single one of those hypotheses panned out. Moreover, most of the nonexperimental findings we have surveyed tested the effectiveness of political advocacy and attack ads *after* campaign consultants, with their superior knowledge, insight, and intuitions, have done everything they can to create the most effective campaign possible for their clients. These nonexperimental studies do not permit us to understand the details of what was done when, but they do point directly to the bottom line of how effective the total campaign strategy was. And, which is important, the nonexperimental studies are no more supportive than the experimental studies of the idea that political attack ads are unusually effective.

A third possibility is that political attack ads used to be unusually effective but no longer are, and, because academic research inevitably lags behind the real-world changes it is trying to understand, we have missed the boat. This idea has the ring of plausibility about it. First, campaign consultants might, over the years, have learned how to combat an opponent's attacks, so that an attack strategy that worked in the 1980s no longer does. It seems to us that we see few examples any more (after the 1988 presidential election) of campaigns in which one candidate "goes negative" and the opponent chooses not to respond in kind. The strongest "test" of the effectiveness (or lack thereof) of attack advertising comes from campaigns in which one candidate employs largely an advocacy strategy, while the opponent chooses largely an attack strategy. But if such campaigns no longer exist—if, whenever one candidate attacks, the opponent almost always quickly retaliates—the two campaigns will roughly match their proportion of attack advertising—but only one of those two campaigns can succeed. Second, the greater effectiveness of political attack advertisements may have been based on their relative rarity—which would lead them to be processed, noticed, and recalled more readily—but as they have become more common, they have become commensurately less effective. Such a "figure-ground" explanation would be consistent with evidence on related topics.[34]

Which, if any, of these accounts is most accurate must remain a matter for speculation at this point. However, it is clear that our prevailing understanding of the effects of political attack ads is in need of fundamental rethinking.

34. Lau (1985).

References

Ansolabehere, Stephen, and Shanto Iyengar. 1995. *Going Negative: How Political Advertisements Shrink and Polarize the Electorate*. Free Press.

Ansolabehere, Stephen, Shanto Iyengar, Adam Simon, and Nicholas Valentino. 1994. "Does Attack Advertising Demobilize the Electorate?" *American Political Science Review* 88 (December): 829–38.

Atkin, Charles, and Gary Heald. 1976. "Effects of Political Advertising." *Public Opinion Quarterly* 40 (summer): 212–28.

Babbitt, Paul R., and Richard R. Lau. 1994. "The Impact of Negative Political Campaigns on Political Knowledge." Paper presented at the annual meeting of the Southern Political Science Association, Atlanta, Ga., November.

Basil, Michael, Caroline Schooler, and Byron Reeves. 1991. "Positive and Negative Political Advertising: Effectiveness of Ads and Perceptions of Candidates." In Frank Biocca, ed., *Television and Political Advertising*. Vol. 1, pp. 245–61. Hillsdale, N.J.: Lawrence Erlbaum.

Berelson, Bernard R., Paul F. Lazarsfeld, and William N. McPhee. 1954. *Voting: A Study of Opinion Formation in a Presidential Campaign*. University of Chicago Press.

Brians, Craig L., and Martin P. Wattenberg. 1995. "The Effects of Political Commercials on Presidential Turnout in 1992." Paper prepared for the annual meeting of the American Political Science Association, Chicago, September.

———. 1996. "Campaign Issue Knowledge and Salience: Comparing Reception from TV Commercials, TV News, and Newspapers." *American Journal of Political Science* 40 (February): 172–93.

Bryce, James. 1889. *The American Commonwealth*. London: Macmillan.

Budesheim, Thomas L., David A. Houston, and Stephen J. DePaola. 1996. "Persuasiveness of In-Group and Out-Group Political Messages: The Case of Negative Political Campaigning." *Journal of Personality and Social Psychology* 70 (March): 523–34.

Bullock, David A. 1994. "The Influence of Negative Political Advertising on Undecided Voters: An Experimental Study of Campaign Message Strategy." Ph.D. diss., Department of Political Science, University of Arizona.

Capella, Louis, and Ronald D. Taylor. 1992. "An Analysis of the Effectiveness of Negative Political Campaigning." *Business and Public Affairs* 18 (Spring): 10–17.

Davis, Michael L., and Michael Ferrantino. 1996. "Towards a Positive Theory of Political Rhetoric: Why Do Politicians Lie?" *Public Choice* 88 (July): 1–13.

Finkel, Steven E., and John Geer. 1998. "A Spot Check: Casting Doubt on the Demobilizing Effect of Attack Advertising." *American Journal of Political Science* 42 (April): 573–95.

Fiske, Susan T., and Shelley E. Taylor. 1991. *Social Cognition*. McGraw-Hill.

Freedman, Paul, and Kenneth M. Goldstein. 1999. "Measuring Media Exposure and the Effects of Negative Campaign Ads." *American Journal of Political Science* 43 (October): 1189–208.

Garramone, Gina M., Charles T. Atkin, Bruce E. Pinkleton, and Richard T. Cole.

1990. "Effects of Negative Political Advertising on the Political Process." *Journal of Broadcasting and Electronic Media* 34 (Summer): 299–311.

Geer, John G., and Richard R. Lau. 1998. "Modeling Campaign Effects: Does Attack Advertising Depress Turnout?" Paper prepared for the ninety-fourth annual meeting of the American Political Science Association, Boston, September.

Goldstein, Kenneth M. 1997. "Political Commercials in the 1996 Election." Paper prepared for the annual meeting of the Midwest Political Science Association, Chicago, April.

Haddock, Geoffrey, and Mark P. Zanna. 1997. "Impact of Negative Advertising on Evaluations of Political Candidates: The 1993 Canadian Federal Election." *Basic and Applied Social Psychology* 19 (June): 204–23.

Hill, Ronald P. 1989. "An Exploration of Voter Responses to Political Advertisements." *Journal of Advertising* 18 (4): 14–2.

Hitchon, Jacqueline C., and Chingching Chang. 1995. "Effects of Gender Schematic Processing on the Reception of Political Commercials for Men and Women Candidates." *Communication Research* 22 (August): 430–58.

Hitchon, Jacqueline C., Chingching Chang, and Rhonda Harris. 1997. "Should Women Emote? Perceptual Bias and Opinion Change in Response to Political Ads for Candidates of Different Genders." *Political Communication* 14 (January): 49–69.

Houston, David A., Kelly Doan, and David Roskos-Ewoldsen. 1999. "Negative Political Advertising and Choice Conflict." *Journal of Experimental Psychology: Applied* 5 (1): 3–16.

Jamieson, Kathleen Hall. 1992. *Dirty Politics: Deception, Distraction, and Democracy*. New York: Oxford University Press.

Kahn, Kim Fridkin, and John G. Geer. 1994. "Creating Impressions: An Experimental Investigation of Political Advertising on Television." *Political Behavior* 16 (March): 93–116.

Kahn, Kim Fridkin, and Patrick J. Kenney. 1999. "Do Negative Campaigns Mobilize or Suppress Turnout? Clarifying the Relationship between Negativity and Participation." *American Political Science Review* 93 (December): 877–89.

Kahneman, Daniel, Paul Slovic, and Amos Tversky, eds. 1982. *Judgment under Uncertainty: Heuristics and Biases*. Cambridge University Press.

Kaid, Lynda Lee. 1997. "Effects of the Television Spot on Images of Dole and Clinton." *American Behavioral Scientist* 40: 1085–95.

Kaid, Lynda Lee, and John Boydston. 1987. "An Experimental Study of the Effectiveness of Negative Political Advertisements." *Communication Quarterly* 35 (Spring): 193–201.

Kaid, Lynda Lee, Mike Chanslor, and Mark Hovind. 1992. "The Influence of Program and Commercial Type on Political Advertising Effectiveness." *Journal of Broadcasting and Electronic Media* 36 (Summer): 303–20.

Kaid, Lynda Lee, Chris M. Leland, and Susan Whitney. 1992. "The Impact of Televised Political Ads: Evoking Viewer Responses in the 1988 Presidential Campaign." *Southern Speech Communication Journal* 57 (Summer): 285–95.

Karrh, James A., and David H. Halpern. 1997. "Nothing to Lose? Assessing the Impact of Competitive Position on Responses to Negative Political Advertising." Paper prepared for the annual conference of the American Academy of Advertising, St. Louis, March.

King, Erika G., and Robert W. Hendersen. 1999. "Effect of Tone of Campaign Ads and Viewers' Initial Attitudes on Ad Efficacy in the 1998 Michigan Gubernatorial Campaign." Paper prepared for delivery at the fifty-seventh annual meeting of the Midwest Political Science Association, Chicago, April.

King, Erika G., Robert W. Hendersen, and Hong C. Chen. 1998. "Viewer Response to Positive vs. Negative Ads in the 1996 Presidential Campaign." Paper prepared for the fifty-sixth annual meeting of the Midwest Political Science Association, Chicago, April.

Laczniak, Gene R., and Clarke L. Caywood. 1987. "The Case for and against Televised Political Advertising: Implications for Research and Public Policy." *Journal of Public Policy and Marketing* 6 (Spring): 16–32.

Lang, Annie. 1991. "Emotion, Formal Features, and Memory for Televised Political Advertisements." In Frank Biocca, ed., *Television and Political Advertising*. Vol. 1, pp. 221–44. Hillsdale, N.J.: Lawrence Erlbaum.

Lau, Richard R. 1985. "Two Explanations for Negativity Effects in Political Behavior." *American Journal of Political Science* 29 (February): 119–38.

Lau, Richard R., Gerald Pomper, and Grace Ann Mumoli. 1998. "Effects of Negative Campaigning on Senate Election Outcomes: 1988, '90, '94, and '96." Paper prepared for the annual meeting of the Midwest Political Science Association, Chicago, April.

Lau, Richard R., Lee Sigelman, Caroline Heldman, and Paul R. Babbitt. 1997. "The Effectiveness of Negative Political Advertisements." Paper presented at the annual meeting of the American Political Science Association, Washington, D.C., August.

———. 1999. "The Effectiveness of Negative Political Advertisements: A Meta-Analytic Assessment." *American Political Science Review* 93 (December): 851–76.

Lazarsfeld, Paul F., Bernard R. Berelson, and Hazel Gaudet. 1948. *The People's Choice*. Columbia University Press.

Lemert, James B., William R. Elliot, James M. Bernstein, William L. Rosenberg, and Karl J. Nestvold. 1991. *News Verdicts, the Debates, and Presidential Campaigns*. Praeger.

Lemert, James B., Wayne Wanta, and Tien-Tsung Lee. 1999. "Party Identification and Negative Advertising in a U.S. Senate Election." *Journal of Communication* 49 (Spring): 123–34.

Luskin, Robert C., and Christopher Bratcher. 1994. "Negative Campaigning, Partisanship, and Turnout." Paper prepared for the annual meeting of the Midwest Political Science Association, Chicago, April.

Martínez, Michael D., and Tad Delegal. 1990. "The Irrelevance of Negative Campaigns to Political Trust: Experimental and Survey Results." *Political Communication and Persuasion* 7 (January/March): 25–40.

Mathews, Douglas, and Beth Dietz-Uhler. 1998. "The Black-Sheep Effect: How

Positive and Negative Advertisements Affect Voters' Perceptions of the Sponsor of the Advertisement." *Journal of Applied Social Psychology* 28 (October): 1903–15.

McBride, Allan, Robert Toburen, and Dan Thomas. 1993. "Does Negative Campaign Advertising Depress Voter Turnout? Evidence from Two Election Campaigns." Unpublished manuscript. Grambling State University, Grambling, La.

McCombs, Maxwell E., and Donald L. Shaw. 1972. "The Agenda-Setting Function of the Mass Media." *Public Opinion Quarterly* 36 (Summer): 176–87.

Merritt, Sharyne. 1984. "Negative Political Advertising: Some Empirical Findings." *Journal of Advertising* 13 (3): 27–38.

Newhagen, John E., and Byron Reeves. 1991. "Emotion and Memory Responses for Negative Political Advertising: A Study of Television Commercials Used in the 1988 Presidential Election." In Frank Biocca, ed., *Television and Political Advertising*. Vol. 1, pp. 197–220. Hillsdale, N.J.: Lawrence Erlbaum.

Pfau, Michael, Henry C. Kenski, Michael Nitz, and John Sorenson. 1989. "Use of the Attack Message Strategy in Political Campaign Communication." Paper prepared for the annual meeting of the Speech Communication Association, San Francisco, November.

Pinkleton, Bruce. 1997. "The Effects of Negative Comparative Political Advertising on Candidate Evaluations and Advertising Evaluations: An Exploration." *Journal of Advertising* 26 (Spring): 19–29.

———. 1998. "Effects of Print Comparative Political Advertising on Political Decision-Making and Participation." *Journal of Communication* 48 (Autumn): 24–36.

Pinkleton, Bruce E., and Gina M. Garramone. 1992. "A Survey of Responses to Negative Political Advertising: Voter Cognition, Affect, and Behavior." *Proceedings of the 1992 Conference of the American Academy of Advertising*, pp. 127–133. Athens, Ga.: American Academy of Advertising.

Putrevu, Sanjay, and Kenneth R. Lord. 1994. "Comparative and Noncomparative Advertising: Attitudinal Effects under Cognitive and Affective Involvement Conditions." *Journal of Advertising* 23 (June): 77–91.

Rahn, Wendy M., and Rebecca Hirshorn. 1999. "Political Advertising and Public Mood: A Study of Children's Political Orientations." *Political Communication* 16 (4): 387–407.

Riker, William H. 1991. "Why Negative Campaigning Is Rational: The Rhetoric of the Ratification Campaign of 1787–1788." *Studies in American Political Development* 5: 224–83.

———. 1997. *The Strategy of Rhetoric: Campaigning for the American Constitution*. Yale University Press.

Roberts, Marilyn S. 1995. "Political Advertising: Strategies for Influence." In Kathleen E. Kendall, ed., *Presidential Campaign Discourse: Strategic Communication Problems*, pp. 179–99. SUNY Press.

Roddy, Brian L., and Gina M. Garramone. 1988. "Appeals and Strategies of Negative Political Advertising." *Journal of Broadcasting and Electronic Media* 32 (Fall): 415–27.

Roese, Neal J., and Gerald N. Sande. 1993. "Backlash Effects in Attack Politics." *Journal of Applied Social Psychology* 23 (August): 632–53.

Schultz, Cindy, and S. Mark Pancer. 1997. "Character Attacks and Their Effects on Perceptions of Male and Female Political Candidates." *Political Psychology* 18 (March): 93–102.

Shapiro, Michael A., and Robert H. Rieger. 1992. "Comparing Positive and Negative Political Advertising on Radio." *Journalism Quarterly* 69 (Spring): 135–45.

Skaperdas, Stergios, and Bernard Grofman. 1995. "Modeling Negative Campaigning." *American Political Science Review* 89 (March): 49–61.

Sulfaro, Valerie A. 1998. "Political Sophistication and the Presidential Campaign: Citizen Reactions to Campaign Advertisements." Paper prepared for the annual meeting of the Midwest Political Science Association, Chicago, April.

Thorson, Esther, William G. Christ, and Clarke Caywood. 1991. "Selling Candidates Like Tubes of Toothpaste: Is the Comparison Apt?" In Frank Biocca, ed., *Television and Political Advertising*. Vol. 1, pp. 145–72. Hillsdale, N.J.: Lawrence Erlbaum.

Thorson, Esther, Ekaterina Ognianova, James Coyle, and Frank Denton. 1996. "Negative Political Ads and Negative Citizen Orientations toward Politics." Unpublished manuscript. University of Missouri, Columbia.

Tinkham, Spencer F., and Ruth Ann Weaver-Lariscy. 1991. "Advertising Message Strategy in U.S. Congressional Campaigns: Its Impact on Election Outcome." *Current Issues and Research in Advertising* 13 (1/2): 207–26.

———. 1993. "A Diagnostic Approach to Assessing the Impact of Negative Political Television Commercials." *Journal of Broadcasting and Electronic Media* 37 (Fall): 377–400.

———. 1994. "Ethical Judgments of Political Television Commercials as Predictors of Attitude toward the Ad." *Journal of Advertising* 23 (September): 43–57.

Wadsworth, Anne Johnston, Philip Patterson, Lynda Lee Kaid, Ginger Cullers, Drew Malcomb, and Linda Lamirand. 1987. "'Masculine' vs. 'Feminine' Strategies in Political Ads: Implications for Female Candidates." *Journal of Applied Communication* 15 (Spring/Fall): 77–94.

Wattenberg, Martin P., and Craig L. Brians. 1999. "Negative Campaign Advertising: Demobilizer or Mobilizer?" *American Political Science Review* 93 (December): 891–99.

Weaver-Lariscy, Ruth Ann, and Spencer F. Tinkham. 1996. "Advertising Message Strategies in U.S. Congressional Campaigns: 1982, 1990." *Journal of Current Issues and Research in Advertising* 18 (Spring): 53–66.

Weigold, Michael F. 1992. "Negative Political Advertising: Individual Differences in Responses to Issue vs. Image Ads." *Proceedings of the 1992 Conference of the American Academy of Advertising*. American Academy of Advertising.

Welch, Susan, and John R. Hibbing. 1997. "The Effects of Charges of Corruption on Voting Behavior in Congressional Elections, 1982–1990." *Journal of Politics* 59 (February): 226–39.

West, Darrell M. 1993. *Air Wars: Television Advertising in Election Campaigns, 1952–1992*. Washington, D.C.: Congressional Quarterly Press.

CHAPTER THREE

Eliminate the Negative? Categories of Analysis for Political Advertisements

KATHLEEN HALL JAMIESON

PAUL WALDMAN

SUSAN SHERR

"IF JEFFERSON IS ELECTED," proclaimed Yale president Reverend Timothy Dwight, "the Bible will be burned, the French 'Marseillaise' will be sung in Christian churches, [and] we will see our wives and daughters the victims of legal prostitution; soberly dishonored; [and] speciously polluted."[1] One might read that statement as confirmation that attack in politics has a long if dishonorable history. Alternatively, it could be interpreted as a caution against taking administrators at Ivy League institutions too seriously.

The problem with Dwight's prophecy is not that it is an attack on Jefferson but that it is inaccurate. Most reporters and many scholars mistakenly assume that "attack" is both "negative" and "dirty." Conflating these terms obscures the important distinction between legitimate and illegitimate attack and minimizes the likelihood that the deceptions found in supposedly "positive" discourse will be probed. Yet in most presidential general elections, deception is as likely in ads and speeches that are self-promotional as in those that are oppositional. In some cases deception is more common in advocacy than in attack ads.

Combining attack with deception is problematic for an additional reason as well. "Negative" political ads that are perceived as truthful elicit more favorable reactions to the sponsor and more unfavorable ones toward the object of attack.[2]

1. Quoted in Coyle (1960), p. 67.
2. Garramone (1984).

44

Since most candidates are not disposed to provide candid appraisals of their own histories and records, the electorate is likely to learn of flaws, faults, and flights of fancy either in press accounts or through attacks by an opponent. Attack serves a second productive purpose when it indicates why one candidate's proposal better meets the country's needs than does another's. Attack is, in other words, a legitimate and important part of differentiating one candidate's biography and positions from another's. As Jamieson argues in *Dirty Politics,* "By dispatching all analysis of an opponent's record, we risk driving engaged comparison and contrast from campaigns entirely."[3] Additionally, as Kahn and Kenney argue in chapter 4, attack also can stimulate learning by voters.

In this chapter we pose two questions that are central to a consideration of negativity in political advertising: how should negativity be defined, and how should the relative amount of negativity in the advertising of a campaign be determined? Specifically, we examine the ways in which scholars have defined negativity and argue that it is desirable to class political ads as attack, advocacy, and contrast. We proceed to make the case that existing analyses of levels of attack or negativity over time suffer from a series of inadequacies. By focusing on "prominent ads" and by dichotomizing ads into negative and positive, scholars have overstated the proportion of attack in political advertising and have misread some election years. We then examine three alternative ways of measuring the level of attack advertising in campaigns: equally weighting the ads on each side, weighting the ads by relative expenditure, and determining the level of attack by multiplying the percentage of attack in the ads for a candidate by the gross ratings points behind the ads and by their duration in seconds. We argue that the last method is the most accurate. Finally, we defend attack and contrastive advertising by showing that the level of policy argument is higher in these two forms than in so-called positive or advocacy ads.

Defining Negativity

Most researchers interested in negativity have parsed political ads into two groups, the positive and the negative (see table 3-1). Although experimental researchers may do so in order to simplify analysis and isolate the

3. Jamieson (1992), p. 220.

Table 3-1. *Definitions of "Negative" as Used in Earlier Academic Studies*

Researcher	Methodology	Unit of analysis	Mode	Taxonomy
Campaign discourse mapping project	Content analysis	Argument	Television	Advocacy, attack, contrast
Ansolabehere and Iyengar (1995)	Experiment	Ad	Television	Positive/negative
Ansolabehere and others (1994)	Experiment	Ad	Television	Positive/negative
Basil, Schooler, and Reeves (1991)	Experiment	Ad	Television	Positive/negative
Christ, Thorson, and Caywood (1994)	Experiment	Ad	Television	Attack/support, image/issue
Faber and Storey (1984)	Survey	Ad	Television	Image/issue/ mudslinging
Finkel and Geer (1998)	Survey	Candidate tone	Television	Positive/negative, trait/issue
Garramone and others (1990)	Experiment	Ad	Television	Positive/negative
Goldstein (1997)	Content analysis	Ad	Television	Positive/negative/ contrast
Hale, Fox, and Farmer (1996)	Content analysis	Ad	Television	Positive/negative
Hill (1989)	Experiment	Ad	Print	Positive/negative/ comparative
Johnson-Cartee and Copeland (1991)	Descriptive	. . .	Television	Positive/negative (direct attack, direct comparison, implied comparison)
Kahn and Geer (1994)	Experiment	Ad	Television	Positive/negative, trait/issue

effects of attack advertising, content analytical work that ignores comparison or contrast overlooks an important and discrete type of discourse.

Implicit in most analyses of negative advertising is the proposition that it is pernicious and we would be better off either without it at all or at least with less of it. We assume instead that attack is a useful component of political discourse and should be encouraged, not discouraged, as long as it is fair, accurate, relevant to governance, and accompanied by advocacy.[4]

We begin by examining commonly used schemes for parsing the nega-

4. Jamieson (1992).

Table 3-1 (continued)

Researcher	Methodology	Unit of analysis	Mode	Taxonomy
Kaid, Chanslor, and Hovind (1992)	Experiment	Ad	Television	Image/issue/ negative
Kaid and others (1993)	Content analysis	Ad	Television	Positive/negative
Kaid and Johnston (1991)	Content analysis	Ad	Television	Positive/negative, others
Kaid, Leland, and Whitney (1992)	Experiment	Ad	Television	Positive/negative
Lang (1991)	Experiment	Ad	Television	Positive/negative
Martínez and Delegal (1990)	Experiment, survey	Ad	Radio	More negative/ less negative
Merritt (1984)	Survey	Ad	Television	Positive/negative
Newhagen and Reeves (1991)	Experiment	Ad	Television	Positive/true negative/ comparative
Pinkleton (1997)	Experiment	Ad	Print	More negative/ less negative
Shapiro and Rieger (1992)	Experiment	Ad	Radio	Positive/negative, image/issue
Thorson, Christ, and Caywood (1991b)	Experiment	Ad	Television	Positive/negative, issue/image
Tinkham and Weaver-Lariscy (1993)	Experiment	Ad	Television	Positive/negative
Tinkham and Weaver-Lariscy (1991)	Survey	Campaign	. . .	Nonpersonal/ positive/negative/ comparative
West (1997)	Content analysis	Ad	Television	Positive/negative

tive. One tradition of research makes inferences about negativity in campaigns from an analysis of press reports. Using that approach, Ansolabehere and Iyengar argue from a small sample (thirty-four states) that attack advertising depresses voter turnout.[5] As a practical matter, however, these scholars do not know whether the campaigns they analyzed had a high, medium, or low level of attack advertising since they make that assumption on the basis of press reports, not content analysis of aired ads.

5. Ansolabehere and others (1994); Ansolabehere and Iyengar (1995).

Although not a study of advertising but rather of negative campaigning, Lau et al. make a similar move—cataloging the percentage of Democratic and Republican negative campaign assertions in news as a way to determine the level of negative campaigning.[6] They conclude that "negative campaigning does not work."

The flaws in this approach are not difficult to isolate. As we have shown elsewhere, the press over-reports attack and under-reports advocacy and contrast when writing about candidate speeches, focusing disproportionately on attack advertising as well.[7] Indeed, one of the problems with ad watches is that they are very likely to be written about attack ads and not likely at all to focus on ads that advocate. Nor does the number of questions that press pollsters ask about campaign negativity bear any clear relationship to the actual level of attack in the ads. And there is no reason to assume that the level of over-reporting of attack is consistent from state to state, study to study. As Lau and Sigelman show in chapter 2 of this volume, many commonly held assumptions about negative advertising— that it is remembered better than positive advertising and that it is more persuasive, for instance—are not borne out by the research in this area. Furthermore, as Finkel and Geer suggest, negative advertising in and of itself does not discourage voter turnout.[8]

A second tradition of inquiry focuses on the actual content of ads. In general this line of research adopts one of three taxonomies. The first and most common categorizes as negative an ad that contains *any* mention of the sponsoring candidate's opponent. This broad definition sweeps all discourse but pure advocacy under the heading "negative." Kaid, Leland, and Whitney, for example, define negative spots as "advertisements that directly refer to an opposing candidate, the issues for which the other candidate stands, or the party of the other candidate."[9] Similarly, Basil, Schooler, and Reeves class an ad as negative when "the ad named the opponent and whether the ad attacked the opponent on position, lying, or running an unfair campaign."[10]

A second category defines as negative those ads that focus *predominantly* on the sponsor's opponent. This scheme also classes ads as either positive or negative, with predominance often left undefined. Ansolabehere

6. Lau, Pomper, and Mazeika (1995).
7. Jamieson, Waldman, and Devitt (1998); Jamieson (1992).
8. Finkel and Geer (1998).
9. Kaid, Leland, and Whitney (1992), p. 287.
10. Basil, Schooler, and Reeves (1991).

and Iyengar classify ads according to "whether the advertisement . . . fo-cuses on a candidate's positive aspects or on the opponent's liabilities and faults," while Kaid and Johnston classify each spot "as positive or nega-tive according to its focus; a negative spot focused on the opposition, and a positive spot focused on the candidate sponsoring the ad."[11] Hale, Fox, and Farmer also define negative advertising as "a predominantly negative portrayal of the opposing candidate's character traits and issue positions."[12]

The final classification system, and the one we believe to be most useful in describing political advertising, adds a third category, that of compari-son or contrast. Included here are ads where the candidate makes claims both in favor of his or her own candidacy and in criticism of his or her opponent. The comparison-contrast category has been used in experiments, a survey study, and content analysis.[13] Table 3-1 provides a general sense of the types of studies falling into these three broad classes. As the table suggests, most researchers working in this area have ignored contrast ads, which in practice make up a substantial portion of candidate advertising.

When we conflate comparison/contrast with attack under the heading of negativity, we blame candidates for offering a form of discourse that is both informative and accountable. Unlike pure attacks, contrastive ads provide accountability, because the ad's sponsor is clearly identifiable. View-ers are provided reasons to vote for as well as against a candidate. In addition, contrastive discourse advances the proposition that political decisionmaking should be based on a weighing of both sides of any issue, encouraging voters to think in more complex terms about their vote. And as we show in this chapter, both attack and comparison/contrast contain a higher level of policy argument than pure advocacy.

The Accuracy of the Collection of Ads

Determining how many attack, contrast, and advocacy ads were aired in a campaign presupposes that one has a full collection of ads and can dis-tinguish those that aired from those that did not. Scholars have been plagued by collections of ads that are incomplete or that do not accurately distin-guish ads that aired from those that did not. Responses to the problem

11. Ansolabehere and others (1994), p. 837; Kaid and Johnston (1991), p. 56.
12. Hale, Fox, and Farmer (1996), p. 335.
13. For experiments, see Newhagen and Reeves (1991) and Hill (1989); for a survey study, see Tinkham and Weaver-Lariscy (1991); and for content analysis, see Goldstein (1997).

have varied. West, for example, codes prominent ads, by which he means ads discussed in Jamieson's *Packaging the Presidency*.[14] That decision biases his analysis toward controversial attack ads.

Those who rely on the archive at the University of Oklahoma base their conclusions on an incomplete collection of presidential general election ads. The archive holds ninety-seven ads from the 1960 campaign, for example, when 122 actually aired. And the collection includes ads that did not air. In 1972, for instance, Tony Schwartz, best known for producing the "Daisy" ad in 1964, was asked to produce a set of ads for the McGovern campaign. He created six ads, some of them in multiple versions. Two of the ads aired nationally; one received a small amount of airing in a single state. Relying on Jamieson's *Packaging the Presidency* as a source, Kaid and Johnston report, "Five spots were produced by Tony Schwartz for McGovern in 1972, but not all were aired nationally. Nonetheless, they were included in this sample because they contributed to an overall, comprehensive view of the campaign."[15] Since they are relying on *Packaging the Presidency* for their information on what did and did not air and that book fails to provide a specific answer, it is probable that what is actually prompting inclusion of all of the ads is an inability to determine which should be counted as airing and which should not. Such information can be extremely difficult to come by, particularly for more distant campaigns. Nonetheless, researchers should hesitate before making historical conclusions based on potentially incomplete data.

The Jamieson archive at the Annenberg School was assembled as the research base for *Packaging the Presidency*. Jamieson determined which ads aired by interviewing the consultants who created them and the time buyers who placed them and also by examining the extant archival records. Those included on the CD-ROM that will be made available to scholars in the spring of 2000 are the ones that aired. This chapter is based on an analysis of those data.

Selection from among Available Ads

To distinguish ads that aired in primaries from those that aired afterward, scholars need to know the approximate date on which the ad first aired.

---

14. West (1993); Jamieson (1996).
15. Jamieson (1996), p. 289; Kaid and Johnston (1991), p. 56.

When comparing across campaigns, an analysis should cover a consistent time frame. In this chapter, we analyze general election ads aired after the beginning of the first major party convention of the year. One problem with this definition is that the date of the first convention varies dramatically from some years to others. The rationale for this time frame is that conventions produce a kind of discourse that focuses on the strengths of the nominee and his party and the weaknesses of the prospective nominee of the other party. Additionally, pollsters traditionally have accepted conventions as a demarcation point when they have asked whether a voter made a voting decision before, during, or after the conventions.

Our Unit of Analysis: The Argument

Unlike previous studies, the Annenberg Campaign Discourse Mapping Project (CDMP) chose as its unit of analysis not the ad but either the idea unit (a phrase, clause, or sentence that carries a claim) or the argument. In its simplest form, an argument consists of a claim plus some evidence or justification for that claim. For example, in the following ad from Bob Dole's 1996 campaign, the claim is "Bill Clinton isn't protecting our children from drugs." The enumeration of Clinton's "failed liberal drug policies" constitutes the evidence for that claim. Together, the claim and evidence are categorized as an argument in the Dole ad:

> The stakes of this election? Our children. Under Clinton, cocaine and heroin use among teenagers has doubled. [evidence] Why? Because Bill Clinton isn't protecting our children from drugs. [claim] He cut the drug czar's office 83 percent. [evidence] Cut 227 drug enforcement agents. [evidence] And cut $200 million to stop drugs at our borders. [evidence]

The first benefit of this unit is that it allows the researcher to examine more closely and more clearly the differing subunits within an individual text. Where many content analyses simply ask what the "predominant" mode of discourse within an ad is, we are able to distinguish different arguments within a given ad. While many thirty-second spots contain only a single argument, longer formats like the five-minute spots common in earlier years are analyzed more accurately argument by argument. Use of argument as a unit of analysis also makes it easier to compare ads to other campaign genres, including speeches and debates.

Weighting the Ads

To isolate patterns in political advertising, the scholar's first step is to decide how ads should be counted and combined. Logic might dictate that a weighting system be based on a standard that differentiates the more important ads from the less important. The likeliest candidate would be airtime: how often each ad was aired and to how many viewers.

Since gathering such information is time-consuming, difficult, and, for earlier presidential campaigns, impossible, for the most part researchers have counted each ad produced by a campaign equally. An alternative to this approach treats each candidate's campaign as an equally weighted whole. In substance, this means that if the challenger aired twenty-five ads and the incumbent aired fifty, each of the challenger's ads would be weighted twice when computing figures for the year as a whole. The principle at work is that if the candidates have bought comparable amounts of airtime, but one candidate has created a larger number of ads, each of those ads should be given a smaller weight. To not make this adjustment in some cases over-represents some forms of discourse.

An example serves to illustrate this problem. In 1980, incumbent Jimmy Carter ran eighty-nine different ads during the general election campaign. Ronald Reagan aired only seventeen, each of which was shown more frequently. Of these, 23 percent of Carter's 100 ad arguments attacked, compared with 44 percent of Reagan's eighteen arguments. If the arguments are simply summed, the advertising as a whole would be calculated as 26 percent negative. However, by averaging the two, we conclude that 34 percent of the advertising attacked. This is a more accurate representation of the advertising seen by voters.

Figure 3-1 shows the results of the first two modifications we have discussed: the inclusion of contrast and the equalization of candidate discourse. For comparison, we also show Kaid and Johnston's and West's trend lines.[16] To update the Kaid and Johnston analysis we include a data point from Kaid for the 1996 campaign.[17] As noted earlier, West relies on ads mentioned in Jamieson's *Packaging the Presidency*.[18]

West's "prominent" ads are in general more negative than the totals obtained by Kaid and by our project. This suggests that the same scholar

16. Kaid and Johnston (1991); West (1993).
17. Kaid (1997).
18. Jamieson (1996).

Figure 3-1. *Attack in Presidential Campaign Ads, 1952–96*[a]

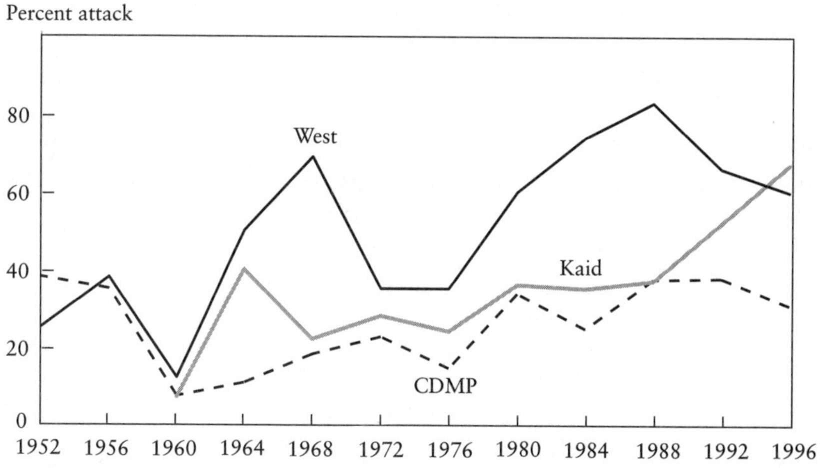

Percent attack

a. CDMP: Campaign discourse mapping project; West: West (1997); Kaid: Kaid and Johnston (1991); Kaid (1997).

who objects to over-reporting the negative in news has over-reported attack ads. Second, we see that, although trends in each of the studies are roughly similar, some significant differences emerge.

The decision to code contrastive advertising as negative, as both Kaid and West do, leads one to overstate the amount of attack. The difference is clearest in 1964, where Kaid's figure for negativity is twenty-nine percentage points higher than the CDMP's, and in 1996, where the difference is thirty-six points. Not coincidentally, those are years with high proportions of contrastive ads. In 1964, most of Barry Goldwater's spots were contrastive. In an apparent move to counter the Lyndon B. Johnson campaign's effort to portray him as reckless, most of the Arizona senator's ads featured the candidate criticizing the Johnson administration, then offering an accompanying proposal for change on the same issue. Likewise, in 1996 more than half of Bill Clinton's ads compared his positions and record to Bob Dole's.

Kaid argues that we will remember the spots in the 1996 campaign as the most negative in history.[19] When one distinguishes between attack ads and contrastive ads, however, we see that five campaigns since 1952 have

19. Kaid (1997).

featured greater amounts of attack than the 1996 race. The following two Clinton spots illustrate the problem with conflating attack with contrast. Although the ads cover similar ground, they differ in both form and focus. The first is a pure attack, offering voters only reasons to vote against Bob Dole. The second contrasts the positions of the two candidates, giving viewers a more complete picture. No fewer than four of Clinton's positions are mentioned. To define this ad as "negative" distorts its actual meaning for the voter. In all, 42 percent of the ads aired in the 1996 general election were contrastive.

Clinton ad: "Adequate"

Announcer: Remember? They shut the government down twice. Newt Gingrich and Bob Dole—they tried to cut Medicare $270 billion, cut education and training $31 billion, deny adequate health care to millions of children. They opposed family and medical leave. Their budget would have forced rural hospital closings. Dole and Gingrich even tried to block a higher minimum wage. Newt Gingrich and Bob Dole. Wrong in the past, wrong for our future.

Clinton ad: "Target"

Announcer: Imagine if Dole and Gingrich were in charge. A hundred-thousand more police. The president's doing it; Dole and Gingrich would undo it. Family and medical leave. The president did it; Dole/Gingrich against. College scholarships. Strengthen education. The president did it; Dole wants to eliminate the Department of Education and undo it. Banning cigarette ads that target children. The president did it. Dole would undo it. Dole/Gingrich: wrong for our future. President Clinton: protecting our values.

The problem with equal weighting is that it assumes that candidates have comparable amounts of money to spend on ads and that they spend those amounts on airtime. This process over-weights the ads of the person who spends less. To correct for this, we need a way to factor amount spent or gross ratings points (GRPs) into the analysis. Since GRPs are not available in early years, dollars spent are the best available surrogate. Although the information available is more precise for some years than for others, it is possible to take the best available data from each year and use them to reweight the ads. The ratios we have calculated are based on data gathered by Jamieson and reported in *Packaging the Presidency*.[20]

20. Jamieson (1996).

Table 3-2. *Ratio of Republican to Democrat Television Ad Expenditures, 1952–76*

Year	Ratio (Republican to Democrat)
1952	10.31 to 1
1956	2.00 to 1
1960	0.81 to 1
1964	1.41 to 1
1968	1.78 to 1
1972	1.02 to 1
1976	0.85 to 1

Source: Jamieson (1996).

Although the amounts vary a bit, we assume that from 1976 to the present the funding available to candidates is roughly equal since in those years both major party candidates received federal financing in the general election.

If we recalculate the figures for attack based on the spending ratios in table 3-2, the trends are altered somewhat (see figure 3-2). A particularly striking difference occurs in 1956, where the amount of attack falls from 35 percent to less than 20 percent. In that year, all of the attack came from Adlai Stevenson, who was outspent by Dwight Eisenhower by more than two to one. By contrast, the figure for 1952 is much higher, since in their first race Eisenhower was the attacker.

In recent years it has been possible to secure the GRP figures indicating the actual audience exposure of ads. In an ideal world from 1996 forward, the sum of GRP multiplied by the percentage of attack multiplied by the duration of ad would be the basis for assessing the level of attack. This time-buy data also would indicate which areas of the country received what mix of candidate advertising. This question is a vital one, particularly for locating advertising effects, since campaigns carefully target their advertising to different areas.[21]

Unit of Analysis: The Idea Unit

Since not all claims in ads are arguments, our focus on argument as a unit of analysis discounts some ad content. As we turn to a discussion of the

21. A project at the Annenberg School has obtained these data for the 1996 presidential campaign; forthcoming publications will report an analysis.

Figure 3-2. *Attack in Campaign Ads, Including Spending Ratio, 1952–96*[a]

Percent attack

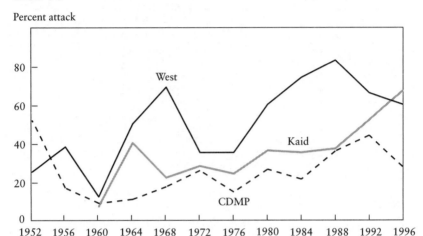

a. CDMP: Campaign discourse mapping project; West: West (1997); Kaid: Kaid and Johnston (1991); Kaid (1997).

policy content present in advertising, we use the idea unit instead of the argument as our unit of analysis. Returning to our distinction among advocacy, contrast, and attack, note that the labels reveal only that an ad consists of attack, advocacy, or, if it is a contrast ad, some combination of the two. An ad composed of 90 percent attack and 10 percent advocacy is a different creature than one that reverses those percentages. To determine what proportion of an ad is advocacy, either we can isolate the arguments in the ad and determine whether they advocate, attack, or contrast or we can make the same judgment about the ad's idea units. We use idea units, not sentences, as our unit of analysis here because some ad claims are found in phrases and clauses that are not complete sentences. So, for example, "100,000 new cops and family and medical leave" would be treated as two idea units. Each idea unit is coded as either advocacy or attack, and the words within each type of unit are summed to create a percentage of each ad that is attack and a percentage that is advocacy.

Since an idea unit is a subset of arguments, but argument is not a subset of idea units, it is possible to code idea units within arguments. Arguments can contain attack, advocacy, or some combination; idea units within ads can be coded for attack, advocacy, or contrast.

Attack and Contrast Ads Carry More Policy Arguments

Political ads contain higher levels of issue information than the public discussion of them would suggest.[22] Indeed, despite the low repute in which they are held, supposedly negative advertisements actually contain more relevant issue content than ads containing no information about the sponsor's opposing candidate.[23] We coded ads produced for presidential campaigns occurring between 1952 and 1996 in order to determine the percentage of policy content found among the different categories of political advertisements. This analysis also allowed us to determine the percentage of policy content in each candidate's arguments and to combine the percentages into a total for each election year.

Statements were coded as policy if they provided information about the difference between candidates' policy positions that would help a voter make an informed voting decision. References to character, "colorful" or scene-setting statements, summative statements introducing or concluding a list of policy statements, and biographical statements were considered nonpolicy. If a policy was mentioned but was preceded by a negative adjective, and no further detail about the policy was articulated, the statement was considered nonpolicy. A reference to Bob Dole's "risky tax scheme" absent further elaboration would be an example of this type of nonpolicy statement. Finally, sentences included in order to further emphasize a point—for example, "you know the result" or "make no mistake about it"—also were considered to be nonpolicy statements.

We coded for policy content 996 individual arguments in general election ads from 1952 to 1996. Only segments running five minutes or shorter in length are included in the database. For the purpose of consistency, longer televised segments are categorized in the database as speeches.

In order to code arguments for policy and nonpolicy content, we used an individual idea unit as the unit of analysis. This analytic scheme resulted in an ability to calculate the amount of policy content as a percentage of total words in arguments in the advertisements, thereby correcting for variations in ad length. Policy content was not calculated for entire ads, only for the arguments found in each ad. Advertisements generally contain only one argument, but some contain more. So, if a spot contained one argument coded as attack and two coded as advocacy, the policy

22. Joslyn (1980); Patterson and McClure (1976).
23. Kaid and Johnston (1991); West (1997).

Figure 3-3. *Average Share of Policy Content, 1952–96*

Percent

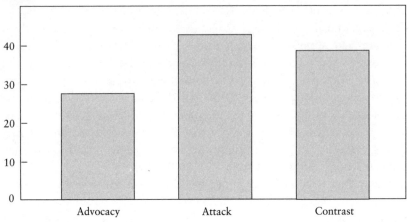

Source: Authors' calculations.

content was calculated for each of these arguments rather than for the ad as a whole. The content analysis was conducted by four coders. Similar to analyses discussed earlier, reliability was greater than the 0.6 level using the stringent Krippendorf reliability alpha.

Consistent with previous studies, our analysis shows that attack advertisements do contain a greater percentage of policy words in argument than advocacy or comparison ads (see figure 3-3). In the ads studied, 42 percent of attack content was coded as policy, as was 39 percent of the contrast content, while only 32 percent of advocacy content was considered policy. This is significant in light of the fact that, in academic and popular discourse, both attack and contrast ads often fall under the pejorative heading negative advertising. Yet both forms offer more policy information to the electorate than the so-called positive ads. Notably, in none of the three categories does the percentage of policy content equal or exceed the percentage of nonpolicy content.

Also, when words found in arguments coded as attack are calculated as a percentage of total words, it becomes clear that attack words make up the smallest percentage of total words in political ads (16 percent). Advocacy arguments comprise the largest portion of total words (53 percent), while contrastive arguments are considerably less prevalent than advo-

Figure 3-4. *Share of Policy Content by Category, 1952–96*

Percent

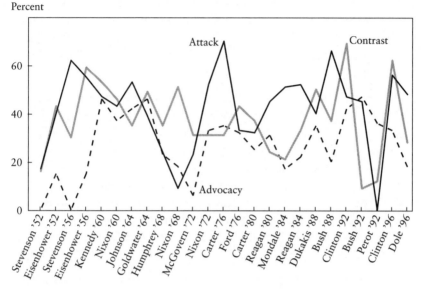

Source: Authors' calculations.

cacy arguments, occupying only 32 percent of the total words. Candidates evidently are devoting the greatest amount of advertising time to the format yielding the least policy discussion. They also are talking about themselves a lot, but devoting less time to discussing their issue positions. This raises the question, should academics and others continue advocating an increase in "positive advertising" without clearly delineating the type of content these ads should contain? It is not enough to be positive. In order to contribute to the deliberative process, an ad should be informative and accurate. Ideally, candidates should be able both to state their own opinions and to criticize those of their opponent without being accused of "going negative."

The percentage of policy content in each argument of each ad category also was calculated for each major candidate running for president between 1952 and 1996 (see figure 3-4). Only in the 1992 Bush campaign did the advocacy category contain the highest percentage of policy words. However, several of the candidates' contrastive arguments contained the highest percentage of policy content. In both 1992 and 1996, President

Clinton produced contrastive advertisements with levels of policy content exceeding 60 percent. In both campaigns, many of Clinton's ads contained lists of his policy positions and initiatives and the contrasting opinions and initiatives of Bush or Dole, a format lending itself to heavy use of policy statements. For example, in 1992, the Clinton campaign ran the following ad:

> *Clinton:* We've been under trickle-down economics for twelve years. Just keep taxes low on the wealthy and see what happens. Well, I'll tell you what's happened. Most Americans are working harder for less money. Unemployment is up. Health care costs are exploding. We are not doing what it takes to compete and win. I've worked hard on a different plan. Let's give incentives to invest in new jobs. Let's spend more on education and training. Let's provide basic health care to all Americans—putting our people first—rebuilding this economy—making us competitive. If we do those things we'll compete and win and we'll bring this country back.

The significance of Clinton's tendency to use contrastive advertising is demonstrated in this analysis. Also significant is the 70 percent policy content of Carter's attack arguments in 1976 compared with the 32 percent policy content in his 1980 attack arguments. This may be attributable to the fact that in 1976 Carter was running against an incumbent with a record.

Conclusions

This analysis demonstrates that the majority of verbal content in political advertisements is not discussion of policy. This result is even more robust in the case of ads that advocate. Although we certainly would hesitate to recommend that candidates use only attack ads in order to increase the amount of policy information presented to voters, it is perhaps equally remiss to promote only advertising that advocates. These data justify our presupposition that the best format for political advertisements is the one used so successfully by Clinton in the last two elections: contrastive advertising.

The content analysis demonstrated that the average contrastive ad contains nearly as high a percentage of policy content as attack ads, making it a better choice than pure advocacy. This format also requires that candidates express their positions on issues while allowing them to criticize their opponents. The contrastive format often presents voters with a choice between two positions on important issues.

Because the phrase "contrast ad" is not common in public discussions of campaigns, defining contrast ads—which both attack and advocate— as a desirable form of discourse has a rhetorical advantage over trying to recast the sense of the public, the press, and the pundits that negativity and attack demean the political process and are bad for the body politic. Although in practice the public seems to distinguish between attack ads that focus on issues and are as a result considered legitimate and those that focus on the traits or personal characteristics of the opposing candidate and are as a result thought to be illegitimate, when asked about direct-reference political ads, negative ads, or attack ads, respondents express widespread disapproval.[24] Surlin and Gordon found that persons of higher social and economic status are more likely than those of middle status to regard direct-reference ads as both unethical and informative.[25] It will, as a result, be easier to secure approval of a "new" concept—the contrast ad—than to rehabilitate two old ones—negativity and attack.

References

Ansolabehere, Stephen, and Shanto Iyengar. 1995. *Going Negative: How Political Advertisements Shrink and Polarize the Electorate*. Free Press.

Ansolabehere, Stephen, Shanto Iyengar, Adam Simon, and Nicholas Valentino. 1994. "Does Attack Advertising Demobilize the Electorate?" *American Political Science Review* 88 (December): 829–38.

Basil, Michael, Caroline Schooler, and Byron Reeves. 1991. "Positive and Negative Political Advertising: Effectiveness of Ads and Perceptions of Candidates." In Frank Biocca, ed., *Television and Political Advertising*. Vol. 1, pp. 245–61. Hillsdale, N.J.: Lawrence Erlbaum.

Christ, William G., Esther Thorson, and Clarke Caywood. 1994. "Do Attitudes toward Political Advertising Affect Information Processing of Televised Political Commercials?" *Journal of Broadcasting and Electronic Media* 38 (3): 251–70.

24. For the distinction between attack ads that focus on issues and attack ads that focus on traits or personal characteristics of the opponent, see Roddy and Garramone (1988); Johnson-Cartee and Copeland (1989); Thorson, Christ, and Caywood (1991b). For direct-reference political ads, see Surlin and Gordon (1977); for negative ads, see Merritt (1984). See also Garramone (1984); Johnson-Cartee and Copeland (1991); Roberts (1992); Pinkleton and Garramone (1992).

25. Surlin and Gordon (1977).

Coyle, David Cushman. 1960. *Ordeal of the Presidency.* Washington, D.C.: Public Affairs Press.

Faber, Ronald, and Claire Storey. 1984. "Recall of Information from Political Advertising." *Journal of Advertising* 13 (3): 39–44.

Finkel, Steven, and John Geer. 1998. "A Spot Check: Casting Doubt on the Demobilizing Effect of Attack Advertising." *American Journal of Political Science* 42 (April): 573–95.

Garramone, Gina M. 1984. "Voter Responses to Negative Ads." *Journalism Quarterly* 61 (2): 250–59.

Garramone, Gina M., Charles T. Atkin, Bruce E. Pinkleton, and Richard T. Cole. 1990. "Effects of Negative Political Advertising on the Political Process." *Journal of Broadcasting and Electronic Media* 34 (Summer): 299–311.

Goldstein, Kenneth. 1997. "Political Advertising and Political Persuasion in the 1996 Presidential Campaign." Paper delivered at the annual meeting of the American Political Science Association, Washington, D.C., August.

Hale, Jon, Jeffrey C. Fox, and Rick Farmer. 1996. "Negative Advertisements in U.S. Senate Campaigns: The Influence of Campaign Context." *Social Science Quarterly* 77 (June): 329–43.

Hill, Ronald. 1989. "An Exploration of Voter Responses to Political Advertisements." *Journal of Advertising* 18 (4): 14–22.

Jamieson, Kathleen Hall. 1992. *Dirty Politics: Deception, Distraction, and Democracy.* New York: Oxford University Press.

———. 1996. *Packaging the Presidency.* New York: Oxford University Press.

Jamieson, Kathleen Hall, Paul Waldman, and James Devitt. 1998. "Mapping the Discourse of the 1996 U.S. Presidential General Election." *Media, Culture, and Society* 20 (2): 347–54.

Johnson-Cartee, Karen S., and Gary Copeland. 1989. "Southern Voters' Reaction to Negative Political Ads in the 1986 Election." *Journalism Quarterly* 66 (4): 888–93, 986.

———. 1991. *Negative Political Advertising: Coming of Age.* Hillsdale, N.J.: Lawrence Erlbaum.

Joslyn, Richard. 1980. "The Content of Political Spot Ads." *Journalism Quarterly* 57 (Summer): 92–98.

Kahn, Kim Fridkin, and John Geer. 1994. "Creating Impressions: An Experimental Investigation of Political Advertising on Television." *Political Behavior* 16 (March): 93–116.

Kaid, Lynda Lee. 1997. "The 1996 Presidential Campaign Spots." *Political Advertising Research Reports* 3 (1): 1.

Kaid, Lynda Lee, Mike Chanslor, and Mark Hovind. 1992. "The Influence of Program and Commercial Type on Political Advertising Effectiveness." *Journal of Broadcasting and Electronic Media* 36 (Summer): 303–20.

Kaid, Lynda Lee, Robert H. Gobetz, Jane Garner, Chris M. Leland, and David K. Scott. 1993. "Television News and Presidential Campaigns: The Legitimization of Televised Political Advertising." *Social Science Quarterly* 74 (2): 274–85.

Kaid, Lynda Lee, and Anne Johnston. 1991. "Negative versus Positive Television Advertising in U.S. Presidential Campaigns, 1960–1988." *Journal of Communication* 41 (Summer): 53–64.

Kaid, Linda Lee, Chris Leland, and Susan Whitney. 1992. "The Impact of Televised Political Ads: Evoking Viewer Responses in the 1988 Presidential Campaign." *Southern Communication Journal* (Summer): 285–95.

Lang, Annie. 1991. "Emotion, Formal Features, and Memory for Televised Political Advertisements." In Frank Biocca, ed., *Television and Political Advertising*. Vol. 1, pp. 221–44. Hillsdale, N.J.: Lawrence Erlbaum.

Lau, Richard R., Gerald Pomper, and Erlinda Mazeika. 1995. "The Effects of Negative Campaigning." Paper presented at the annual meeting of the American Political Science Association, Chicago, September.

Martínez, Michael E., and Tad Delegal. 1990. "The Irrelevance of Negative Campaigns to Political Trust: Experimental and Survey Results." *Political Communication and Persuasion* 7 (January/March): 25–40.

Merritt, Sharyne. 1984. "Negative Political Advertising: Some Empirical Findings." *Journal of Advertising* 13 (3): 27–38.

Newhagen, John, and Byron Reeves. 1991. "Emotion and Memory Responses for Negative Political Advertising: A Study of Television Commercials Used in the 1988 Presidential Election." In Frank Biocca, ed., *Television and Political Advertising*, vol. 1, pp. 197–220. Hillsdale, N.J.: Lawrence Erlbaum.

Patterson, Thomas, and Robert McClure. 1976. *The Unseeing Eye.* Putnam.

Pinkleton, Bruce. 1997. "The Effects of Negative Comparative Political Advertising on Candidate Evaluations and Advertising Evaluations: An Exploration." *Journal of Advertising* 26 (Spring): 19–29.

Pinkleton, Bruce, and Gina Garramone. 1992. "A Survey of Responses to Negative Political Advertising: Voter Cognition, Affect, and Behavior." In L. N. Reid, ed., *Proceedings of the 1992 Conference of the American Academy of Advertising*, pp. 127–33. Athens, Ga.: American Academy of Advertising.

Roberts, Marilyn S. 1992. "The Fluidity of Attitudes toward Political Advertising." In L. N. Reid, ed., *Proceedings of the 1992 Conference of the American Academy of Advertising*, pp. 134–43. Athens, Ga.: American Academy of Advertising.

Roddy, Brian, and Gina Garramone. 1988. "Appeals and Strategies of Negative Political Advertising." *Journal of Broadcasting and Electronic Media* 32 (Fall): 415–27.

Shapiro, Michael, and Robert Rieger. 1992. "Comparing Positive and Negative Political Advertising on Radio." *Journalism Quarterly* 69 (Spring): 135–45.

Surlin, S. H., and T. F. Gordon. 1977. "How Values Affect Attitudes toward Direct-Reference Political Advertising." *Journalism Quarterly* 54 (1): 89–98.

Thorson, Esther, William Christ, and Clarke Caywood. 1991a. "The Effects of Issue-Image Strategies, Attack and Support Appeals, Music, and Visual Content in Political Commercials." *Journal of Broadcasting and Electronic Media* 35 (4): 465–86.

———. 1991b. "Selling Candidates Like Tubes of Toothpaste: Is the Comparison Apt?" In Frank Biocca, ed., *Television and Political Advertising*, vol. 1, pp. 145–72. Hillsdale, N.J.: Lawrence Erlbaum.

Tinkham, Spencer, and Ruth Ann Weaver-Lariscy. 1991. "Advertising Message Strategy in U.S. Congressional Campaigns: Its Impact on Election Outcome." *Current Issues and Research in Advertising* 13 (1/2): 207–26.

———. 1993. "A Diagnostic Approach to Assessing the Impact of Negative Political Television Commercials." *Journal of Broadcasting and Electronic Media* 37 (Fall): 377–99.

West, Darrell. 1993. *Air Wars: Television Advertising in Election Campaigns, 1952–1992.* Washington, D.C.: Congressional Quarterly Press.

———. 1997. *Air Wars: Television Advertising in Election Campaigns, 1952–1996,* 2d ed. Washington, D.C.: Congressional Quarterly Press.

CHAPTER FOUR

How Negative Campaigning Enhances Knowledge of Senate Elections

KIM FRIDKIN KAHN

PATRICK J. KENNEY

AT THE HEART OF self-government in the United States is the ability of citizens to determine who holds political power. Citizens make decisions about who should govern after a formal campaign period where representatives and their rivals publicly discuss and debate the critical issues of the day. These debates serve to empower individuals with information so they can decide whom they want to govern their lives. In order for voters to exercise their role in a representative democracy, they must be afforded political discourse that is composed of reflective, critical, and reasoned debates about important matters facing the nation.[1]

Today, there are increasing worries that America's campaigns fall far short of providing citizens with the information necessary to evaluate the merits of competing candidates and their policy proposals. One aspect of campaigns that has received intense scrutiny is the tenor of political debates. In particular, practitioners, politicians, and political scientists bemoan the increasing negativity of political campaigns. Some pundits claim that negative ads are "debasing democracy" and "wreak[ing] havoc on

The names of the authors appear in alphabetical order because this chapter is in every way a collaborative enterprise. A portion of the data for this chapter were made available through the Inter-University Consortium for Political and Social Research, University of Michigan. Of course, the consortium bears no responsibility for the analyses herein. The data on advertising, news, and campaign managers were supported with a grant from the National Science Foundation (SBR-9308421)

1. Guttman (1993).

our nation's psyche and sense of purpose."[2] J. H. Clinger, in an article in the *Journal of Law and Politics*, goes so far as to say that negative political advertising has led to an "increasing intellectual and ethical bankruptcy of modern political debate" and that the "very future of democratic self-government may be threatened."[3] To be sure, these are serious claims.

Negative campaigning is not a new phenomenon; it has been part of American politics for 200 years. The 1998 mid-term elections were no exception. Negative campaigning was perhaps most conspicuous in the New York Senate race where Senator Alfonse D'Amato (R) was challenged by Representative Charles E. Schumer (D). As we saw in chapter 2, the race included relentless attacks by both candidates on a wide variety of topics, including the candidates' voting records, ethics, and political ideology. D'Amato used Schumer's voting record of twenty-three years to portray the Brooklyn representative as too liberal and openly hostile to upstate New York. Schumer's attacks on D'Amato were just as negative. Schumer's main charge was that D'Amato was a chronic liar. To promote this theme, Schumer concluded most of his attack commercials with the tag line, "Too many lies for too long." As Adam Nagrouney, a reporter for the *New York Times,* explained, "the sharpness of the attacks, the sheer volume, and the mix of positive and negative commercials" made the New York race the most negative of 1998.[4]

Although the American public is familiar with these types of attacks, questions remain concerning the impact that negative campaigns have on the electorate. In this chapter we examine some unexplored consequences of negative campaigning. We begin with a short review of the existing empirical evidence. The majority of studies examining negative advertising have focused on how ads influence voters' views of the competing candidates.[5]

More recently, a growing literature explores the relationship between negative commercials and participation in elections.[6] Although some of these studies suggest that negative advertisements demobilize the elector-

2. Kamber (1997), p. 12, and Goodman (1995), p. 22, respectively.

3. Clinger (1987), pp. 746–47.

4. Adam Nagourney, "Candidates Risk Little with Harsh Ads," *New York Times,* October 13, 1998, p. B5.

5. For a thorough review, see Lau and Sigelman (chapter 2 of this volume).

6. Ansolabehere and Iyengar (1995); Ansolabehere and others (1994); Finkel and Geer (1998); Goldstein (1997); Kahn and Kenney (1999a).

ate, others find that negative commercials do not dissuade people from voting and may actually motivate people to participate in elections.[7]

A few studies have examined the effect of negative advertisements on citizens' attitudes about the political process more generally.[8] Similar to the work focusing on participation, these studies have produced conflicting findings. For example, negative advertisements appear to depress voters' feelings of civic duty, yet they do not seem to alter citizens' trust in the political system.

Based on existing evidence, we cannot confidently conclude that negative political advertisements are harmful to our electoral process. As Lau and Sigelman demonstrate in chapter 2 of this volume, the debate centering on the consequences of negative campaigning is far from settled. In this chapter, we push the literature in a somewhat different direction. We examine a largely unexplored topic concerning negative commercials: Do potential benefits arise from the use of negative advertising? We have reasons to believe that the answer is yes. In particular, we hypothesize that negative commercials create a more informed citizenry. We contend that individuals learn more about candidates and political issues when they receive negative messages than when they receive positive messages. To explore this topic, we examine the messages disseminated by senatorial candidates. We look at the content and tone of candidates' messages in U.S. Senate elections and rely on the National Election Study's Senate Election Study (NES/SES) to determine what voters know about the competing candidates.

Why Negative Commercials Inform the Electorate

Although citizens often complain about the harshness of critical commercials, they find negative advertisements more memorable than commercials focusing on candidates' strengths.[9] Negative political advertising may be easy to remember because negative information is unique, making it

7. For the first type of studies, see Ansolabehere and Iyengar (1995); Ansolabehere and others (1994). For the second type, see Finkel and Geer (1998); Goldstein (1997); Kahn and Kenney (1999a).

8. For example, see Ansolabehere and Iyengar (1995); Clinger (1987); Martínez and Delegal (1990).

9. Basil, Schooler, and Reeves (1991); Lang (1991); Newhagen and Reeves (1991).

more likely to be noticed and more likely to be processed.[10] Lau explains that most people, most of the time, live in a positive world.[11] We are satisfied with our family, our neighborhood, and our job. Against this positive backdrop, negative information stands out because it is relatively rare.

Since negative information is unexpected, it is more credible and more informative. Given this "perceptual explanation," when people are bombarded with political commercials, they pay greater attention to negative advertisements than to positive ones. Since they focus more intensely on these critical commercials, they are more likely to remember the information contained in negative advertisements.

Negative information also may be more memorable because people often are motivated to avoid costs rather than to achieve gains.[12] Research by social psychologists shows that potential costs influence decisions more often than potential gains in decisionmaking situations, ranging from simple bets, to ethical risk taking, to "life dilemma" situations.[13]

In the political realm, citizens may be more motivated to avoid electing ineffective, immoral, or dishonest politicians than to support knowledgeable, upstanding, and trustworthy candidates. If this is the case, then people may pay more attention to negative arguments than to information emphasizing the candidates' strengths in order to avoid making a costly mistake. Thus we expect negative commercials to generate more interest and attention than positive commercials. And we hypothesize that people's understanding of the electoral campaign and its political contestants will increase if they are exposed to campaigns featuring a higher proportion of negative commercials than if they are exposed to campaigns with more positive commercials.

Design

To examine whether the tone of political commercials is related to people's understanding of political contests, we need to integrate information about people's knowledge of political contests with information about the types

10. Kanouse and Hanson (1972); Lau (1982, 1985); McGraw and Steenbergen (1997); Richey and others (1982).

11. Lau (1982).

12. Kanouse and Hanson (1972); Lau (1982); McGraw and Steenbergen (1997).

13. Kahneman and Tversky (1979); Kanouse and Hanson (1972); Lau (1982, 1985). Lau and Sigelman's review of the literature in chapter 2 of this volume suggests that negative ads are not always more memorable than positive ads.

of advertisements disseminated during campaigns. We achieve this integration for the population of U.S. Senate races contested between 1988 and 1992. We rely on the 1988–92 NES/SES for data about respondents' knowledge of their state's senatorial candidates. As Krasno points out, the NES/SES is "unique because, like the Senate itself, it includes (roughly) equal numbers of respondents from all fifty states."[14] National surveys, in contrast, are problematic because most respondents in a nationwide survey are drawn from the largest states, leading to an overrepresentation of competitive Senate contests.[15]

About sixty respondents in each state were randomly selected to be interviewed for the NES/SES. The interviews were done by telephone and took place within two months of the 1988, 1990, and 1992 elections. In total, 9,253 interviews were completed, with 3,145 respondents interviewed in 1988, 3,349 respondents in 1990, and 2,759 respondents in 1992. The interviews averaged just over thirty-five minutes in length.

The NES/SES included a number of questions tapping respondents' knowledge of the campaign, including measures assessing the respondent's ability to recall and recognize the candidates' names, the respondent's ability to rate the candidates on a liberal-conservative ideological scale, and the respondent's ability to identify the major themes of campaigns. In addition, like all National Election Study surveys, respondents were asked a number of political (for example, party identification) and demographic (for example, level of education) questions.

To complement the NES/SES data, we collected data assessing the tone of the candidates' commercials in each Senate race. We examined *televised* political advertisements because these commercials are a central component of U.S. Senate campaigns. Today, all Senate campaigns employ television advertising, if feasible financially.[16] Ansolabehere, Behr, and Iyengar found that television advertising represents the single biggest expenditure by Senate candidates.[17] Furthermore, television advertisements are considered significantly more effective than newspaper advertisements at swaying voters' opinions.[18]

---

14. Krasno (1994), p. 10.
15. Krasno (1994); Mann and Wolfinger (1980); Westlye (1991).
16. Herrnson (1995); Krasno (1994).
17. Ansolabehere, Behr, and Iyengar (1993).
18. Abramowitz and Segal (1992); Goldenberg and Traugott (1984); Jacobson (1997); Luntz (1988).

We relied on the Political Commercial Archive at the University of Oklahoma to obtain our sample of political commercials. The archive has the largest collection of U.S. Senate ads publicly available.[19] The number of advertisements available for candidates involved in contested races in 1988, 1990, and 1992 varied widely. Some candidates produced considerably more ads than others. We stratified the population of ads by candidate and randomly selected four advertisements (if available) for each of the candidates running for the U.S. Senate in 1988, 1990, and 1992. We only examined advertisements that were aired by the candidates. This maximized the number of candidates represented in our sample of political advertisements.

The final sample consisted of 594 ads representing 161 candidates. We obtained 266 advertisements for seventy of the eighty incumbents seeking reelection and 209 advertisements for fifty-eight of the eighty challengers. We sampled 119 advertisements for thirty-three of the thirty-four candidates seeking to fill open seats. The sample included 364 ads from Republican candidates and 230 from Democratic candidates. Finally, of the 594 ads, 33 percent aired in 1988, 32 percent appeared in 1990, and 35 percent aired in 1992.[20]

To measure the tone of the commercials, we followed the work of previous scholars and placed ads into one of seven categories: (1) positive ads about the candidate's views on the issues, (2) positive ads about the candidate's traits, (3) negative ads about the opponent's views on the issues, (4) negative ads about the opponent's traits, (5) ads comparing the candidates on the issues, (6) ads comparing the candidates on their personal traits, and (7) ads presenting a mixture of positive and negative themes.[21] In our analyses, we relied on a ratio of negative ads to all other ads to determine the proportion of negative advertisements present in the campaign setting. Specifically, we divided the number of negative commercials by the total number of commercials examined for each race.[22]

---

19. In contrast, Jamieson, Waldman, and Sherr (chapter 3 of this volume) consider the Jamieson Archive at the Annenberg School to be superior for studying presidential campaigns.

20. Three coders were sent to the archive in Oklahoma. All coders worked separately at the archive. Of the ads that were coded, 25 percent were coded by all three coders to assess reliability. Intercoder reliability among the three coders averaged 80 percent across the ads.

21. For example, see Joslyn (1980); Kaid and Davidson (1986); Kaid and Sanders (1978).

22. In terms of the categorization of commercials discussed above, negative advertisements are those falling into categorizes 3, 4, 5, 6, or 7.

Senate campaigns provide an ideal laboratory for examining the impact of negative messages. Compared with presidential races, Senate races provide a significantly greater number of elections to study. While presidential elections are few in number (one occurs only every four years), one-third of all Senate seats are contested every two years. The election years of 1988, 1990, and 1992 provide ninety-seven contested U.S. Senate campaigns for analysis. In contrast, examining all presidential campaigns since the advent of political advertising in 1952 yields only twelve cases for analysis.

In addition, Senate races are more heterogeneous than both presidential races and House races. Campaigns for the U.S. Senate vary greatly in the amount of money spent, the quality of the candidates, and the content and tone of candidates' messages.[23] For example, Finkel and Geer's analysis of presidential campaigns shows that presidential races have been primarily negative since 1980.[24] In Senate races, in contrast, some candidates refrain completely from negative advertising, while others air only negative commercials.

In summary, by combining the NES/SES data with information about the candidates' advertisements, we can look at the relationship between campaign tone and citizens' levels of information across a large number of races. With this design, we can examine whether negative commercials produce a more knowledgeable citizenry.

An Overview of Candidates' Negative Advertisements

We begin our analysis by describing the nature of negative information in U.S. Senate campaigns. Based on our sample of political advertisements, we find that 41 percent of all advertisements contain criticisms of the opponent. As figure 4-1 illustrates, the percentage of negative commercials increases dramatically for nonincumbents compared with incumbents. For example, while more than half of the challengers' advertisements are negative, less than one-third of the incumbents' commercials are categorized as critical. This is expected because challengers need to explain to potential voters why the sitting senator should be replaced.

The data in figure 4-1 also indicate that Democrats and Republicans are equally likely to use negative advertisements during their campaign

23. For example, Franklin (1991); Kahn and Kenney (1999b); Westlye (1991).
24. Finkel and Geer (1998).

Figure 4-1. *Share of Negative Commercials by Candidate Status, Candidate Party, and Competitiveness of the Race*[a]

Percent of negative commercials

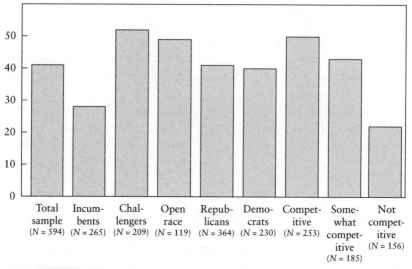

Total sample (N = 594)	Incumbents (N = 265)	Challengers (N = 209)	Open race (N = 119)	Republicans (N = 364)	Democrats (N = 230)	Competitive (N = 253)	Somewhat competitive (N = 185)	Not competitive (N = 156)

a. The numbers are the percentage of the candidates' commercials categorized as negative. Races are categorized as competitive if less than fifteen points separate the candidates in pre-election polls, races are somewhat competitive if between fifteen and twenty-nine points separate the candidates in pre-election polls, and races are noncompetitive if thirty or more points separate the candidates in pre-election polls. The number in parentheses is the number of advertisements analyzed for each category.

for the U.S. Senate. However, as campaigns become more competitive (local polls report the race as too close to call), candidates of both parties dramatically increase their reliance on negative advertisements. When candidates are involved in noncompetitive races (thirty or more points separate the candidates in local polls), negative messages constitute only 22 percent of the candidates' advertisements. However, as the competitiveness of the race increases, candidates are much more likely to depend on negative commercials. In the most competitive races, half of the candidates' advertisements are negative.

When candidates decide to attack, they either criticize their opponent's personal traits (for example, my opponent lacks integrity) or they criticize their opponent's policy views. When focusing on issues, candidates often discuss their opponent's positions on the issues. They identify the rival's positions by producing legislative votes, examining statements in speeches

Figure 4-2. *Share of Commercials Criticizing the Candidates' Policy Positions and Blaming the Opponent for Unfavorable Policy Outcomes*[a]

Percent

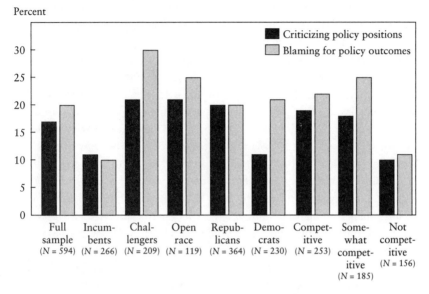

a. The numbers are the percentage of the candidates' commercials categorized as negative. Races are categorized as competitive if less than fifteen points separate the candidates in pre-election polls, races are somewhat competitive if between fifteen and twenty-nine points separate the candidates in pre-election polls, and races are noncompetitive if thirty or more points separate the candidates in pre-election polls. The number in parentheses is the number of advertisements analyzed for each category.

and commercials, and following responses to reporters' questions. In addition to drawing attention to their opponent's policy views, candidates also blame their opponent for unfortunate policy consequences. For example, if a candidate's opponent voted frequently to increase funding for social programs while in Congress, then the attacking candidate may blame the opponent for increasing the size of the national debt.

In our sample of advertisements, candidates criticize their opponent's policy stands in 17 percent of their ads, and they blame their rival for unfavorable policy outcomes 20 percent of the time. As the data in figure 4-2 illustrate, nonincumbents rely on these negative appeals far more than incumbents do. These differences make sense because incumbents have a public record that can be used as fodder for generating criticisms.

The data in figure 4-2 also show that Republicans are more likely than Democrats to attack their opponent's positions on the issues. During the period between 1988 and 1992, more Americans viewed themselves as conservative than as liberal.[25] Wisely, Republicans took advantage of public opinion to criticize their Democratic opponents on a series of issue positions linked to traditionally liberal ideas (for example, creating a large centralized government in Washington in order to solve social problems).

Finally, and as expected, candidates in competitive races are more likely to criticize their opponent's positions on issues. Similarly, candidates contesting close races are more likely to produce advertisements blaming their opponent for unfavorable policy outcomes. For example, when politicians are running in races where thirty or more points separate the candidates in the polls, they rely on the "blaming" strategy only 11 percent of the time. However, reliance on this strategy doubles when candidates are running in the most competitive contests.

Just as candidates choose between different issue strategies when attacking their opponent, candidates who decide to criticize their opponent on character traits also can select from various options. The data in figure 4-3 show that candidates emphasize a variety of negative traits in their commercials. The first four categories (incompetent, lacks leadership, insensitivity, lacks integrity) correspond to Kinder's four trait dimensions (competence, leadership, integrity, and empathy).[26] The next two categories tap criticisms of the opponent's record and behavior in the U.S. Senate or other political offices (negative Washington ties and negative voting record). The "lacks background" category contains comments questioning the opponent's qualifications for the U.S. Senate, and "negative campaigning" includes criticisms of the opponent for pursuing negative campaigns. Finally, we have included an "other category" for negative personal themes not encompassed in the eight previous categories.

The data reveal that when Senate candidates decide to attack the personal traits of a rival, they spend a lot of time criticizing their opponent's behavior in office, with complaints about connections in Washington generating the most discussion. Candidates also criticize their opponent's voting record in almost one-quarter of their negative advertisements.

In contrast, attacks on a candidate's character are less common. Of the negative personal messages, 14 percent raise questions about the opponent's integrity. Advertisements attacking a candidate's competence, leadership ability, and sensitivity are even less common.

25. Kahn and Kenney (1999b).
26. Kinder (1986).

Figure 4-3. *Negative Traits Stressed in Negative Political Advertisements*[a]

Percent stressing negative traits

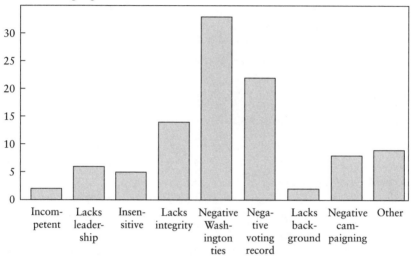

a. The "incompetent" category includes negative references to the following traits: knowledgeable, intelligent, effective, competent, independent, hardworking. The "lacks leadership" category includes negative references to the following traits: inspiring, strong leader. The "insensitive" category includes negative references to the following traits: compassionate, sensitive, nice person, ties with state, and trustworthiness. The "negative Washington ties" category includes negative comments about the candidate's behavior in Washington, D.C. (for example, House bank overdrafts, frequent use of honoraria, ties to Washington-based interest groups, abuses of office privileges). "Negative voting record" includes criticisms of the candidate's record in elective office (for example, absenteeism, votes hurting the state's interests, flip-flops in voting). The "lacks background" category includes negative references to the candidate's political experience. The "negative campaigning" category includes criticisms of the candidate for running a negative campaign. The numbers in this figure are based on the sample of negative commercials (N = 129).

The negative traits emphasized by candidates do not vary by the candidate's party or the level of competition in the race. Although not pictured in figure 4-3, calculations reveal that incumbents and nonincumbents concentrate on different traits when attacking their opponent. In particular, nonincumbents are more likely to use the senator's tenure in Washington as a liability. Challengers, for example, discuss their opponent's Washington ties in a negative light almost half of the time (47 percent). In contrast, incumbents attack their opponent's Washington ties only 11 percent of the time.

In summary, candidates are equally likely to use trait and issue attacks when developing negative campaign advertisements. When candidates choose to attack their opponent on the issues, they often attack issue positions or blame the opponent for unpopular policy outcomes. Republicans are more likely than Democrats to attack their opponent's policy stands, and nonincumbents are more likely than incumbents to develop commercials blaming their opponent for unfavorable policy outcomes. When attacking the opponent on personal traits, candidates often attack the opponent's voting record or ties to the Washington establishment.

The Impact of Negative Advertising on Voters' Level of Information

In this section we examine whether the candidates' negative messages inform voters. In particular, do voters learn more about campaigns and candidates when candidates rely more heavily on critical commercials than on more positive advertisements? To assess this possibility we control for several rival forces that may affect voters' level of information about candidates and campaigns.

Principal among these are the characteristics of citizens. A large body of research has isolated several factors that influence people's level of information about campaigns specifically and about politics more generally. These factors include citizens' repository of information about politics, citizens' reliance on the news media for information, citizens' interest in politics, citizens' psychological attachment to one of the political parties, and citizens' educational background.[27] Not surprisingly, research confirms that people who have a base of knowledge about politics, who follow political events in the news, who are interested in campaigns, who are partisan by nature, and who are better educated are more informed about contemporary campaigns. Clearly, we need to control for these characteristics before we can make claims about the influence of negative ads on people's understanding of the senatorial campaigns in their state.[28]

27. On citizens' repository of information about politics, see Converse (1962, 1964); Dalager (1996); Krosnick (1990); on citizens' reliance on the news media for information, see Brians and Wattenberg (1996); Drew and Weaver (1991); Larson (1990); Zhao and Chaffee (1995); on citizens' interest in politics, see Dalager (1996); McLeod and McDonald (1985); Robinson and Davis (1990); on citizens' psychological attachment to one of the political parties, see Miller and Shanks (1996); and on citizens' educational backgrounds, see Rosenstone and Hansen (1993).

28. See the measurement appendix for a description of how each control variable is operationalized.

Beyond the varying abilities and predispositions of voters, the characteristics of the candidates also may influence people's knowledge about the political contestants. People are likely to know more about senior senators as well as experienced challengers.[29] In addition, candidates who are embroiled in scandals may be better known than candidates who have steered clear of such controversies.[30] And the gender of the candidates may affect what people know about the Senate contestants.[31] Similar to the characteristics of the voters, we need to control for the characteristics of candidates.

Finally, certain campaigns are more interesting and more engaging than others. The campaign environment alters what voters may or may not know about the candidates. For example, citizens do not receive the total sum of their campaign information directly from the candidates. The news media play an important role in disseminating information to would-be voters.[32] Consequently, the amount of campaign information disseminated by the news media will affect people's understanding of the senatorial contests. When more paragraphs are written about a given Senate race, citizens are likely to be better informed.

In addition, competitive campaigns also are likely to motivate citizens to acquire and retain more information about the contest and its rival candidates than low-key campaigns where polls suggest that one candidate will coast to easy victory.[33] Similarly, campaigns with high levels of spending by the candidates may produce a more informed electorate since candidates spend their money trying to convince voters of their virtues, while pointing out the foibles of their opponent. Candidates spend money in a variety of ways, such as airing commercials, staging rallies, sending mailers, and trying to attract news coverage for their candidacy.[34]

Having taken these rival explanations into account, we turn to exploring whether negative commercials alter voters' level of knowledge about the candidates. To assess what voters know about the candidates and campaigns, we turn to a series of measures provided by the NES/SES.

29. Krasno (1994).

30. Abramowitz and Segal (1992).

31. Kahn (1996). Even at this late date, women seeking high elective office are rare. Voters unaccustomed to seeing women compete for the U.S. senate may be more likely to take notice when the campaign is something other than the typical male versus male contest.

32. Graber (1996).

33. Kahn and Kenney (1999b); Krasno (1994); Westlye (1991).

34. We do not distinguish between incumbent and candidate spending because we are interested in capturing the total amount of campaign activity in each race.

Recognition and Recall of the Candidates' Names

The most fundamental piece of information voters need to know during campaigns is the names of the candidates. In the NES/SES survey from 1988 to 1992, 96 percent of respondents recognized the name of the incumbent senator in their home state, while 77 percent recognized the names of the challengers. With regard to the tougher task of recalling the names of the candidates, 75 percent recalled the incumbent's name, while only 56 percent provided interviewers with the challenger's name.[35] We expect citizens' knowledge about the names of the competing candidates to vary systematically with the number of negative advertisements disseminated during the campaign, all other things being equal.

In appendix table 4A-1, we examine whether the negativity of the candidates' advertisements influences citizens' familiarity with the candidates.[36] We also look at whether the respondents' background, the characteristics of the candidates, and the characteristics of the campaign environment influence voters' knowledge of the candidates. As we can see from the logit coefficients, the tone of campaign advertisements affects people's knowledge of the challenger, but not of the incumbent. The positive and significant coefficient in the challenger model indicates that, as the proportion of negative commercials increases, citizens are *more* likely to recognize and recall the name of the challenger. For incumbents, the tone of the commercials is statistically unrelated to people's ability to recall the incumbent's name.

Therefore, negative advertisements actually serve as a resource for challengers. When people are presented with more negative commercials, they become significantly more aware of the challenger's name, even controlling for a host of rival forces.

Additional campaign characteristics, such as the amount of campaign

35. We analyze incumbents and winners in open races in one category and challengers and losers in open races in a second category. We combine these races because there were only seventeen open races from 1988 to 1992. To be certain that this decision does not bias the analysis, we include a measure for open races to see if respondents' level of information about open candidates is different from their information about candidates contesting incumbent seats.

36. Since the dependent variable is dichotomous, we use the more efficient logistic regression analysis to estimate the model rather than ordinary least squares. We do not examine recognition for incumbents in table 4A-1 because of the restricted variance associated with the dependent variable (that is, 96 percent of the respondents recognized the names of the incumbents).

spending, the closeness of the polls, and the amount of news coverage, greatly affect people's knowledge of the challenger. These campaign factors are not as important for predicting recall of the incumbent's name. For instance, the closeness of the race is among the most important factors predicting recall of the challenger. In contrast, the competitiveness of the race is not related to recall of the incumbent. These findings have face validity because most challengers enter campaigns virtually unknown to voters. Incumbents, in contrast, are familiar to many citizens long before the start of the campaign.

The characteristics of respondents are strongly related to whether people recognize and recall the candidates' names. In each of the models, sophistication, attention to the news, interest, and education are related to voters' ability to recognize the candidates, with political sophistication being the most consequential.[37]

The characteristics of the candidates also affect people's knowledge of the candidates. In the models predicting recall and recognition of the challenger, we find that challengers with more experience are more familiar to respondents. Similarly, as senators become more senior, people are more likely to recall their name. Senators who have been embroiled in scandal also enjoy greater familiarity, most likely for the wrong reasons. Finally, people are more likely to recall the names of women senators and women challengers than those of their male colleagues.

Willingness to Make Ideological Judgments

Acquiring the names of the competing candidates is a rudimentary fact that citizens need before they can process more complicated information about the candidates, such as issue positions, personal characteristics, and ideological profiles. In this section, we probe whether citizens hold information beyond the simplest facts about candidates and whether their knowledge is related to the proportion of negative ads presented during the campaign. In particular, we look at whether the tone of commercials affects citizens' likelihood of placing candidates on the ideological spectrum.

Ideological placement of candidates is a more difficult task for citizens than simply recognizing and recalling candidates' names. In the NES/SES,

37. Beta coefficients are useful for examining the relative strength of a variable in any given model. However, beta coefficients are only useful for making comparisons within samples. Thus these standardized coefficients cannot be used to compare our findings with those of other samples.

80 percent of the respondents offer an ideological score for incumbents, while only 59 percent place challengers on the ideological scale. In the analysis presented in appendix table 4A-2, we examine whether people's likelihood of making an ideological judgment is affected by the type of commercials presented during the campaign.[38] If negative advertisements are more interesting, engaging, and memorable, then negative commercials may encourage people to make ideological evaluations of the candidates.

The logit analysis presented in table 4A-2 demonstrates that commercials affect people's willingness to place challengers on the ideological scale. As the proportion of negative advertisements in a race escalates, people are more willing to place the challenger on the left-right spectrum. In fact, the negativity of commercials is more important for understanding respondents' likelihood of making ideological judgments about challengers than many of the remaining variables in the model, including education, media use, strength of party attachment, and interest in campaigns.

In contrast, the tone of political commercials does not affect people's ability to place the incumbent on the same ideological scale. Similarly, other campaign characteristics, such as campaign spending, standing in the polls, and amount of news coverage of the race, fail to reach statistical significance in the incumbent model. Each of these indicators, however, is quite important for predicting respondents' willingness to place the challenger on the ideological scale.

To explain people's willingness to place incumbents on the ideological scale, it is more important to understand the background of respondents (for example, political sophistication, interest in politics, education, and attention paid to the news media) and the characteristics of the incumbent (for example, seniority, involvement in a scandal, and gender). Among these factors, political sophistication is the most influential. The standardized coefficient for political sophistication is more than six times larger than any other variable in the incumbent model.

Although the characteristics of the respondents and candidates are statistically significant in the model predicting willingness to place challengers on the ideological scale, the standardized coefficients are consistently smaller in the challenger model than in the incumbent model. Clearly, the campaign is more important for understanding what people know about challengers.

38. The dependent variable is whether the respondent placed the candidate on the ideological scale. Since the dependent variable is dichotomous, we used logistic regression to estimate the model.

Knowledge of Campaign Themes

Thus far, we have shown that the tone of political commercials affects people's knowledge of challengers. As the proportion of negative advertisements increases, respondents become increasingly likely to recognize and recall the challenger's name. Negative commercials also increase the likelihood that respondents will make ideological judgments about challengers. In this section, we look at whether the negativity of the candidates' commercials affects citizens' knowledge of campaign themes.

During campaigns, candidates spend a great deal of money and effort trying to identify and implement effective campaign themes. If these themes are to be persuasive, citizens need to be able to identify the main thrust of the messages. In this analysis we look at whether candidates are successful at disseminating their messages to citizens. Specifically, as the proportion of negative advertisements increases, are respondents more likely to identify negativity as a main theme of the campaign? To examine this topic, we rely on the following question asked during the NES/SES survey: "In your state, what issue did the candidates talk about the most during the campaign for the Senate?"[39] If respondents mentioned "negativity" or "mudslinging" as the most discussed issue, respondents are given a score of 1. All remaining answers are coded 0. Of the respondents, 8 percent said that "negativity" was the main issue of the campaign.

The analysis in appendix table 4A-3 illustrates that citizens are sensitive to the tenor of the candidates' messages. As the proportion of negative commercials escalates, citizens become increasingly more likely to mention "negativity" as the main issue of the campaign. The negativity of political commercials is among the strongest predictors in the model, performing better than nine of the thirteen remaining variables.

In addition to the tone of the candidates' commercials, the closeness of the race powerfully affects people's impressions of the campaign. As races become more competitive, people are much more likely to mention negativity as a main theme of the campaign. The characteristics of respondents also influence whether people mention the negativity of the campaign. Citizens who are more politically sophisticated, more interested in politics, and more educated are more likely to describe the campaign as nega-

39. The question does not single out issues according to incumbents or challengers, but rather treats the candidates together. Thus the analyses relying on this question do not compare incumbents and challengers. Nevertheless, the question provides a rich source of data about whether voters were able to learn about the campaign.

tive. Similarly, people who pay more attention to the news media recognize negative campaigns more than other respondents do. Finally, people who are weakly attached to the political parties mention negativity as a campaign theme more often than strong partisans.

In our final analysis, we look at whether the negativity of the candidates' commercials affects whether citizens *accurately* describe the themes of the campaign. In other words, as the proportion of negative commercials in a campaign increases, are respondents more likely to correctly identify the candidates' major themes?

We rely on a telephone survey of campaign managers to identify the candidates' main themes. We examine whether respondents mention these themes when asked about the main issues of the campaign.[40] Only 19 percent of the respondents correctly named one of the main themes of the Senate campaign. However, the analysis in appendix table 4A-4 demonstrates that the tone of the candidates' commercials affects dramatically people's ability to identify the campaign's main themes. In fact, the tone of the commercials is more important than any of the other variables in the model, with the exception of seniority.

To illustrate the importance of the tone of commercials, we convert the logit coefficients in table 4A-4 to probabilities that are more readily interpretable.[41] Using this procedure, we find that people living in states where only positive commercials are aired have a 0.29 probability of correctly identifying the themes of the campaign. However, people are much more adept at recalling the themes of the campaigns when candidates rely on negative advertisements. In particular, respondents living in states where all the commercials are negative have a 0.44 probability of correctly identifying the candidates' major themes.

Not surprising, the amount of news published about the race also affects people's likelihood of recalling the main messages of the campaign. However, the remaining campaign variables—the closeness of the race

40. We interviewed campaign managers for each of the major-party candidates running for election to the U.S. senate in 1988, 1990, and 1992. We completed interviews with 76 percent of the managers. During the interview, campaign managers were asked to identify the main themes of their campaign. We coded up to six responses for each candidate. For a more complete description of the campaign manager survey, see Kahn and Kenney (1999b). In this analysis, we examine only races where interviews were completed with both campaign managers. This yielded a sample of 3,653 respondents.

41. In calculating these probabilities, we relied on the procedure described in King (1989) by varying the campaign tone and holding all the remaining variables in the model at their means.

and the amount of money spent by the candidates—are not related to people's ability to correctly identify the main themes.

The characteristics of respondents, although not as important as the tone of candidates' commercials, also affect whether people identify the candidates' themes. As before, citizens with more political sophistication, education, and interest are better able to identify the main themes of a campaign. In addition, people who follow the news media regularly are adept at identifying the themes disseminated by the candidates.

Finally, the characteristics of the candidates influence respondents' likelihood of recalling the main themes of a campaign. Seniority is the most influential. The negative sign suggests that voters are less likely to identify the themes of senior senators. This is understandable because senior incumbents tend to shy away from clear-cut policy themes.[42]

Overall, the results of our analysis demonstrate that negative advertising produces a more informed electorate. As the proportion of negative advertising increases, citizens become more knowledgeable about the campaign.[43] People learn more about the challenger, and their awareness of the themes of the campaign increases dramatically.[44]

42. Kahn and Kenney (1999b).

43. Given Jamieson, Waldman, and Sherr's (chapter 3 of this volume) distinction between attack and contrast ads, we analyzed the impact of two additional advertising variables. First, we computed the proportion of contrast ads (to all other ads) in each race, relying on Jamieson, Waldman, and Sherr's definition. In particular, contrast ads are ads where a candidate makes claims both in favor of his or her own candidacy and in criticism of his or her opponent. We included this contrast variable in each of the analyses presented in tables 4A-1–4A-4 (in lieu of the proportion of negative ads). We found that the proportion of contrast ads failed to significantly increase awareness ($p < 0.05$) in each analysis. Second, we computed the proportion of attack ads (to all other ads) in each race. Attack ads, according to Jamieson, Waldman, and Sherr, are ads focusing entirely on the sponsoring candidate's opponent. We include the attack variable in each analysis, while omitting the proportion of all negative ads. We find that the results for attack ads are very similar to the results for our original measure (proportion of all negative ads). The proportion of attack ads significantly increased awareness in five of the seven analyses.

44. We conducted two additional analyses to see if the substance of the negative advertisement influenced learning during the campaign. First, we looked at the proportion of negative trait advertisements (to all other ads). When we included this variable (and excluded the variable measuring the proportion of all negative ads), we found that the proportion of negative trait ads significantly increases awareness in only two of the seven analyses ($p < 0.05$). Finally, we looked at whether the proportion of negative issue advertisements influenced learning during campaigns. The negative issue variable significantly increases learning in only two of the seven logit analyses ($p < 0.05$). These results suggest that the original measure—the proportion of all negative ads in a race—is the superior measure.

Conclusions

Pollster Mark Mellman, a staunch defender of negative advertising, explained that, "When we ask people about negative ads, they'll say they don't like them. But that's not the point. The point is they absorb the information."[45] According to our analysis, Mellman is correct. People do learn from negative advertising. As the proportion of negative advertising in a campaign increases, people become more informed about the candidates and their messages.

Negative advertising is particularly important for challengers. As campaigns become more negative, citizens are more likely to recall and recognize the challenger's name, and they are more likely to place the challenger on the left-right ideological scale. The tone of campaign commercials is less influential for incumbents. Incumbents are better known than challengers because of their history of service to the state. For sitting senators, the negativity of the campaign commercials does not influence people's knowledge of their candidacy.

The tone of political commercials also influences people's familiarity with the messages of the campaign. As the proportion of commercials becomes more negative, people are increasingly likely to mention "negativity" as a main theme of the campaign. Similarly, people are more likely to correctly identify the candidates' campaign themes when they witness races with numerous negative advertisements.

Although pundits and scholars often criticize negative advertisements as harmful to the Democratic process, our research suggests that negative advertisements can be beneficial. Negative advertisements, more so than positive advertisements, increase people's understanding of campaigns and candidates. If an informed electorate is a desirable outcome of campaigns, then negative advertisements may perform an important function in our electoral system.

Finally, the findings in this study raise normative questions concerning the nature of the negative information that voters receive from candidates. Our findings indicate clearly that citizens are more likely to remember information if it is presented in a critical fashion. But at what cost? What if the candidates' messages are full of distortions intended to mislead potential supporters? Do opponents and the news media counter these false accusations so that the disseminators pay at the ballot box for their

45. Salmore and Salmore (1989), p. 33.

slander? Is there a point where harsh and shrill criticisms disgust voters so they withdraw from the political process? It is not enough for us to discover that negative political messages increase understanding of the campaign; it is imperative to investigate other potential consequences of these negative communications. The nature of political discourse in campaigns and its consequences remain central features of representative democracies and are worthy of extended study.

Table 4-A1. *Logit Analysis Explaining Recognition and Recall of the Candidates*[a]

	Incumbent recall		Challenger recall		Challenger recognition	
Characteristic	Unstandardized coefficient	Beta	Unstandardized coefficient	Beta	Unstandardized coefficient	Beta
Campaign characteristic						
Advertising tone	−0.08 (0.06)[b]	0.04	0.22** (0.07)	0.13	0.44** (0.08)	0.27
Campaign spending	0.04** (0.008)	0.14	0.07** (0.009)	0.28	0.16** (0.01)	0.68
Closeness of race	0.0002 (0.001)	0.01	−0.01** (0.001)	−0.40	−0.008** (0.001)	−0.34
Amount of news	0.0002** (0.00003)	0.23	0.0003** (0.00004)	0.38	0.0005 (0.00006)	0.69
Respondent characteristic						
Interest	0.12** (0.01)	0.35	0.11** (0.01)	0.36	0.10** (0.01)	0.36
Political sophistication	0.22** (0.01)	0.70	0.23** (0.01)	0.83	0.12** (0.01)	0.46
Strength of party	0.01 (0.01)	0.02	0.01 (0.01)	0.02	−0.0004 (0.02)	−0.001
Education	0.05** (0.005)	0.31	0.05** (0.006)	0.36	0.03** (0.005)	0.23
Attention to news	0.03** (0.003)	0.25	0.03** (0.004)	0.29	0.02** (0.004)	0.21
Candidate characteristic						
Challenger's experience	—	—	0.03** (0.006)	0.19	0.05** (0.008)	0.34
Gender	0.10** (0.04)	0.08	0.16** (0.04)	0.14	−0.03 (0.04)	−0.03
Scandal	0.10** (0.05)	0.06	—	—	—	—
Seniority	0.01** (0.002)	0.16	—	—	—	—
Open	−0.12** (0.05)	−0.09	−0.07 (0.04)	−0.06	0.03 (0.05)	0.03
Constant	−1.94** (0.12)		−2.25** (0.15)		−0.35** (0.15)	
Percentage correctly predicted	70		78		80	
Number of cases	6,110		6,110		6,110	

— Variable not included in analysis.

** *p* < 0.01.

a. Recall is a binary variable where 1 = respondent recalls the candidate's name; 0 = otherwise. Recognition is a binary variable where 1 = respondent recognizes the candidate's name; 0 = otherwise. Advertising tone is the proportion of negative commercials, ranging from 0 (no negative commercials) to 1 (all commercials are negative). Campaign spending is the amount of money spent per voter during the campaign. Closeness of the race is the difference in poll standings between the candidates, ranging from 0 to 72. Amount of news is the number of paragraphs published about the race in the largest circulating newspaper. Interest is measured on a three-point scale. Political sophistication is based on a six-point scale. Strength of party is measured on a four-point scale, ranging from independent (1) to strong partisan (4). Education is measured by years of schooling. Attention to news is measured on a fourteen-point scale. Challenger's experience is measured on a nine-point scale. Gender is a binary variable where 1 = female candidate; 0 = male candidate. Scandal is a binary variable where 1 = candidate involved with a scandal; 0 = otherwise. Seniority is measured by years in the U.S. Senate. Open is a binary variable where 1 = incumbent race; 0 = open race. All *p*-values are based on two-tailed tests.

b. Numbers in parentheses are standard errors.

Table 4-A2. *Logit Analysis Explaining Willingness to Place Candidates on Ideological Scale*[a]

Characteristic	Incumbent ideology		Challenger ideology	
	Unstandardized coefficient	Beta	Unstandardized coefficient	Beta
Campaign characteristic				
Advertising tone	−0.15 (0.09)[b]	0.20	0.15** (0.07)	0.17
Campaign spending	0.008 (0.01)	0.09	0.05** (0.009)	0.40
Closeness of race	0.0004 (0.002)	0.04	0.01** (0.001)	0.81
Amount of news	0.00003 (0.00004)	0.09	0.00009** (0.00004)	0.33
Respondent characteristic				
Interest	0.06** (0.01)	0.46	0.04** (0.01)	0.26
Political sophistication	0.45** (0.01)	2.99	0.24** (0.01)	1.72
Strength of party	0.02 (0.02)	0.11	0.04** (0.01)	0.19
Education	0.01** (0.006)	0.16	0.002 (0.004)	0.03
Attention to news	0.02** (0.004)	0.44	−0.00004 (0.004)	0.01
Candidate characteristic				
Challenger's experience	—	—	0.02** (0.006)	0.25
Gender	0.19** (0.05)	0.40	0.13** (0.03)	0.24
Scandal	0.15** (0.06)	0.23	—	—
Seniority	0.008** (0.003)	0.34	—	—
Open	−0.04 (0.06)	0.08	−0.14** (0.04)	0.24
Constant	−1.19** (0.14)	−0.43	−0.43** (0.12)	
Percent correctly predicted	96		92	
Number of cases	6,110		6,110	

— Variable not included in analysis.

** $p < 0.01$.

a. Ideology is a binary variable where 1 = respondent is willing to place the candidate on ideology scale; 0 = otherwise. Advertising tone is the proportion of negative commercials, ranging from 0 (no negative commercials) to 1 (all commercials are negative). Campaign spending is the amount of money spent per voter during the campaign. Closeness of the race is the difference in poll standings between the candidates, ranging from 0 to 72. Amount of news is the number of paragraphs published about the race in the largest circulating newspaper. Interest is measured on a three-point scale. Political sophistication is based on a six-point scale. Strength of party is measured on a four-point scale, ranging from independent (1) to strong partisan (4). Education is measured by years of schooling. Attention to news is measured on a fourteen-point scale. Challenger's experience is measured on a nine-point scale. Gender is a binary variable where 1 = female candidate; 0 = male candidate. Scandal is a binary variable where 1 = candidate involved with a scandal; 0 = otherwise. Seniority is measured by years in the U.S. Senate. Open is a binary variable where 1 = incumbent race; 0 = open race. All p-values are based on two-tailed tests.

b. Numbers in parentheses are standard errors.

Table 4A-3. *Logit Analysis Examining Whether Respondents Mention Negativity as a Campaign Theme*[a]

Characteristic	Unstandardized coefficient	Beta
Campaign characteristic		
Advertising tone	0.32** (0.11)[b]	0.30
Campaign spending	−0.01 (0.01)	0.06
Closeness of race	−0.01** (0.002)	0.93
Amount of news	−0.00005 (0.00005)	0.10
Respondent characteristic		
Interest	0.04** (0.02)	0.22
Political sophistication	0.13** (0.02)	0.76
Strength of party	−0.09** (0.02)	0.34
Education	0.03** (0.009)	0.35
Attention to news	0.01* (0.006)	0.16
Candidate characteristic		
Challenger's experience	0.02** (0.009)	0.21
Gender	0.003 (0.07)	0.004
Scandal	0.11 (0.07)	0.12
Seniority	−0.002 (0.003)	0.06
Open	−0.09 (0.08)	0.12
Constant	−1.57** (0.21)	
Percent correctly predicted	92	
Number of cases	6,110	

* $p < 0.05$.
** $p < 0.01$.

a. Negativity mentioned is a binary variable where 1 = respondent mentioned "negativity" as a campaign theme; 0 = otherwise. Advertising tone is the proportion of negative commercials, ranging from 0 (no negative commercials) to 1 (all commercials are negative). Campaign spending is the amount of money spent per voter during the campaign. Closeness of the race is the difference in poll standings between the candidates, ranging from 0 to 72. Amount of news is the number of paragraphs published about the race in the largest circulating newspaper. Interest is measured on a three-point scale. Political sophistication is based on a six-point scale. Strength of party is measured on a four-point scale, ranging from independent (1) to strong partisan (4). Education is measured by years of schooling. Attention to news is measured on a fourteen-point scale. Challenger's experience is measured on a nine-point scale. Gender is a binary variable where 1 = female candidate; 0 = male candidate. Scandal is a binary variable where 1 = candidate involved with a scandal; 0 = otherwise. Seniority is measured by years in the U.S. Senate. Open is a binary variable where 1 = incumbent race; 0 = open race. All p-values are based on two-tailed tests.

b. Numbers in parentheses are standard errors.

Table 4A-4. *Logit Analysis Explaining Whether Respondents Correctly Identify Campaign Theme*[a]

Characteristic	Unstandardized coefficient	Beta
Campaign characteristic		
Advertising tone	0.66** (0.10)[b]	0.35
Campaign spending	0.01 (0.01)	0.04
Closeness of race	−0.002 (0.002)	−0.08
Amount of news	0.0002** (0.00004)	0.21
Respondent characteristic		
Interest	0.08** (0.02)	0.24
Political sophistication	0.08** (0.01)	0.22
Strength of party	−0.008 (0.02)	−0.02
Education	0.02** (0.007)	0.13
Attention to news	0.01** (0.005)	0.12
Candidate characteristic		
Challenger's experience	−0.02** (0.008)	−0.13
Gender	0.29** (0.05)	0.28
Scandal	0.15** (0.06)	0.11
Seniority	-0.03** (0.003)	−0.51
Open	0.31** (0.07)	0.27
Constant	-0.74** (0.17)	
Percent correctly predicted	76	
Number of cases	3,653	

* $p < 0.05$.
** $p < 0.01$.

a. Correct identification of a campaign theme is a binary variable where 1 = respondent correctly identified the campaign theme, 0 = respondent incorrectly identified the campaign theme. Advertising tone is the proportion of negative commercials, ranging from 0 (no negative commercials) to 1 (all commercials are negative). Campaign spending is the amount of money spent per voter during the campaign. Closeness of the race is the difference in poll standings between the candidates, ranging from 0 to 72. Amount of news is the number of paragraphs published about the race in the largest circulating newspaper. Interest is measured on a three-point scale. Political sophistication is based on a six-point scale. Strength of party is measured on a four-point scale, ranging from independent (1) to strong partisan (4). Education is measured by years of schooling. Attention to news is measured on a fourteen-point scale. Challenger's experience is measured on a nine-point scale. Gender is a binary variable where 1 = female candidate; 0 = male candidate. Scandal is a binary variable where 1 = candidate involved with a scandal; 0 = otherwise. Seniority is measured by years in the U.S. Senate. Open is a binary variable where 1 = incumbent race; 0 = open race. All *p*-values are based on two-tailed tests.

b. Numbers in parentheses are standard errors.

Appendix B. Measurement Appendix

This appendix describes our method of measuring the characteristics of campaigns, respondents, and candidates. It is designed to help students understand the operationalization of key concepts and to help scholars replicate our work.

Campaign Characteristics

Amount of news. We measure the amount of news with a content analysis of the largest circulating newspaper in the state. In particular, we count the number of paragraphs written about the campaign from September 1 through election day.[46]

Campaign spending. To measure campaign spending, we calculate the total amount of spending by the candidates during the course of the campaign. We then divide the amount of campaign spending by voting-age population so that we can make sensible comparisons of expenditures across populous states and small states (for example, California and New York versus Wyoming and Idaho).

Closeness of Senate elections. To measure the closeness of Senate elections, we rely on polling data taken from two sources: (1) the content analysis of state newspapers and (2) Campaign Hotline, a political archive. These polls were published during the last month of the campaign. The closeness of the race is calculated by coding the percentage difference between the two candidates in the polls. For example, if 52 percent of citizens preferred one candidate, while 42 percent preferred the second candidate, then the race is given a score of 10 percent (that is, $52 - 42 = 10$). In our sample, closeness ranges from 0 (no difference in support for the candidates) to 72 (seventy-two points separate the candidates according to the poll).

Respondent Characteristics

Attention to news. To assess attention to the news, we rely on the NES/SES questions asking voters how often during a week they watched a news program on television or read a newspaper. We combine these two measures into one index tapping attention to the news. The two questions were "How many days in the past week did you watch news programs on TV?" and "How many days in the past week did you read a daily newspa-

---

46. For more information about this content analysis, see Kahn and Kenney (1999b).

per?" Thus the index ranges from 0 to 14, with 14 representing an individual who reports reading a newspaper every day and watching a news program every day.

Education. This is an interval measure based on the question "What is the highest grade of school or year of college you have completed?"

Interest. To measure interest, we use the NES/SES question, "Some people don't pay much attention to political campaigns. How about you? Would you say that you are very much interested, somewhat interested, or not much interested?" Respondents who replied "very much interested" received a score of 3; respondents who were "somewhat interested" received a score of 2; the remaining respondents received a score of 1.

Political sophistication. We rely on answers to six questions to measure political sophistication. Following Zaller, we examine "correct" comparative placements of George Bush and the Democratic and Republican parties on the seven-point liberal-conservative continuum.[47] The respondent's answer is coded as correct if a respondent said George Bush or the Republican party was moderate to extremely conservative. Similarly, if the respondent said the Democratic party was moderate to extremely liberal, the answer is coded as correct.

We also measure respondents' level of information about the senator not up for reelection in the state, since information about the senator seeking reelection is contaminated by the ongoing campaign. We use the following three NES/SES measures to assess knowledge of the senator not seeking reelection: correct recognition of the senator's name, correct recall of the senator's name, and correct ideological placement of the senator. To measure correct ideological placement, we recode Americans for Democratic Action (ADA) scores to range from 1 to 3 (1 = liberal; 2 = moderate; 3 = conservative) and average the scores for the two years prior to the respondent's interview date. Each respondent's answer to the ideological placement of the senator also is recoded from 1 to 3 (1 = liberal; 2 = moderate; 3 = conservative). If the difference between the respondent's recoded score and the recoded ADA score is 0, the respondent correctly identified the ideological placement of the senator. If the score is different from 0, the respondent incorrectly identified the ideological placement of the senator.

Strength of party. The standard seven-point party identification question is recoded into four categories: 0 = independent, 1 = leaning partisan, 2 = weak partisan, and 3 = strong partisan.

---

47. Zaller (1992).

Candidate Characteristics

Challenger's experience. The quality of the challenger is measured using prior elective experience and establishing a nine-point scale. Following prior work by Squire, we rank nonincumbents accordingly: 1 = no prior elective experience; 2 = no prior elective experience, but high name recognition due to celebrity status in the state; 3 = local electoral experience; 4 = state legislator; 5 = state legislative leader; 6 = mayor of a major city; 7 = first-term statewide office holder or member of U.S. House of Representatives; 8 = multiple-term statewide office holder or member of U.S. House of Representatives; 9 = governor.[48]

Scandal. We follow Abramowitz's conception of scandal by identifying special circumstances as reported by *Congressional Quarterly's* October "Election Preview."[49] Candidates involved in a scandal receive a score of 1; all other candidates receive a score of 0.

Seniority. An incumbent's seniority is measured as number of years in the Senate.

Open races. Races between an incumbent and a challenger receive a score of 1; races between two nonincumbents receive a score of 0.

References

Abramowitz, Alan I. 1988. "Explaining Senate Election Outcomes." *American Political Science Review* 82 (June): 385–403.

Abramowitz, Alan I., and Jeffrey A. Segal. 1992. *Senate Elections.* University of Michigan Press.

Ansolabehere, Stephen, Roy Behr, and Shanto Iyengar. 1993. *The Media Game: American Politics in the Television Age.* Macmillan.

Ansolabehere, Stephen, and Shanto Iyengar. 1995. *Going Negative: How Political Advertisements Shrink and Polarize the Electorate.* Free Press.

Ansolabehere, Stephen, Shanto Iyengar, Adam Simon, and Nicholas Valentino. 1994. "Does Attack Advertising Demobilize the Electorate?" *American Political Science Review* 88 (4): 829–38.

Basil, Michael, Caroline Schooler, and Byron Reeves. 1991. "Positive and Negative Political Advertising: Effectiveness of Ads and Perceptions of Candidates." In Frank Biocca, ed., *Television and Political Advertising.* Vol. 1: *Psychological Processes.* Hillsdale, N.J.: Lawrence Erlbaum.

48. Squire (1989, 1992).
49. Abramowitz (1988).

Brians, Craig L., and Martin P. Wattenberg. 1996. "Campaign Issue Knowledge and Salience: Comparing Reception from TV Commercials, TV News, and Newspapers." *American Journal of Political Science* 40 (1): 172–93.

Clinger, J. H. 1987. "The Clean Campaign Act of 1985: A Rational Solution to Negative Campaign Advertising Which the One-Hundredth Congress Should Reconsider." *Journal of Law and Politics* 3 (3): 727–48.

Converse, Philip E. 1962. "Information Flow and Stability of Partisan Attitudes." *Public Opinion Quarterly* 26 (4): 578–99.

———. 1964. "Nature of Belief Systems in Mass Publics." In David Apter, ed., *Ideology and Discontent.* Free Press.

Dalager, Jon K. 1996. "Voters, Issues, and Elections: Are the Candidates' Messages Getting Through?" *Journal of Politics* 58 (2): 486–515.

Drew, Dan, and David Weaver. 1991. "Voter Learning in the 1988 Presidential Elections: Did the Debates and the Media Matter?" *Journalism Quarterly* 68 (1/2): 27–37.

Finkel, Steven, and John Geer. 1998. "A Spot Check: Casting Doubt on the Demobilizing Effect of Attack Advertising." *American Journal of Political Science* 42 (2): 573–95.

Franklin, Charles H. 1991. "Eschewing Obfuscation? Campaigns and the Perceptions of U.S. Senate Incumbents." *American Political Science Review* 85 (4): 1193–214.

Goldenberg, Edie N., and Michael W. Traugott. 1984. *Campaigning for Congress.* Washington, D.C.: Congressional Quarterly Press.

Goldstein, Kenneth. 1997. "Political Advertising and Political Persuasion in the 1996 Presidential Campaign." Paper delivered at the annual meeting of the Midwest Political Science Association, Chicago, April.

Goodman, Adam. 1995. "Producing TV: A Survival Guide." *Campaigns & Elections* 16 (7): 22–24.

Graber, Doris. 1996. *Mass Media and American Politics.* Washington, D.C.: Congressional Quarterly Press.

Guttman, Amy. 1993. "The Disharmony of Democracy." In John W. Chapman and Ian Shapiro, eds., *Democratic Community.* New York University Press.

Herrnson, Paul S. 1995. *Congressional Elections: Campaigning at Home and in Washington.* Washington, D.C.: Congressional Quarterly Press.

Jacobson, Gary C. 1997. *The Politics of Congressional Elections.* Longman.

Joslyn, Richard. 1980. "The Content of Political Spot Ads." *Journalism Quarterly* 57 (Summer): 92–98.

Kahn, Kim F. 1996. *The Political Consequences of Being a Woman: How Stereotypes Influence the Content and Impact of Statewide Campaigns.* Columbia University Press.

Kahn, Kim F., and Patrick J. Kenney. 1999a. "Do Negative Campaigns Mobilize or Suppress Turnout? Clarifying the Relationship between Negativity and Participation." *American Political Science Review* 93 (4): 877–89.

———. 1999b. *The Spectacle of U.S. Senate Campaigns.* Princeton University Press.

Kahneman, Daniel, and Amos Tversky. 1979. "Prospect Theory: An Analysis of Decision under Risk." *Econometrica* 47 (2): 263–91.

Kaid, Lynda L., and Dorothy K. Davidson. 1986. "Elements of Videostyle: Candidate Presentations through Television Advertising." In Lynda L. Kaid, Dan Nimmo, and Keith R. Sanders, eds., *New Perspectives on Political Advertising*. Southern Illinois University Press.

Kaid, Lynda Lee, and Keith R. Sanders. 1978. "Political Television Commercials: An Experimental Study of Type and Length." *Communication Research* 5 (1): 57–70.

Kamber, Victor. 1997. *Poison Politics: Are Negative Campaigns Destroying Democracy?* Plenum Press.

Kanouse, David E., and L. Reid Hanson Jr. 1972. "Negativity in Evaluations." In Edward E. Jones, David E. Kanouse, Harold H. Kelley, Richard E. Nisbett, Stuart Valins, and Bernard Weiner, eds., *Attribution: Perceiving Causes of Behavior*. Morriston, N.J.: General Learning Press.

Kinder, Donald R. 1986. "Presidential Character Revisited." In Richard R. Lau and David O. Sears, eds., *Political Cognition*. Hillsdale, N.J.: Lawrence Erlbaum.

King, Gary. 1989. "Variance Specification in Even Count Models: From Restrictive Assumptions to a Generalized Estimator." *American Journal of Political Science* 33 (3): 762–84.

Krasno, Jonathan S. 1994. *Challengers, Competition, and Reelection: Comparing Senate and House Elections*. Yale University Press.

Krosnick, Jon A. 1990. "Expertise and Political Psychology." *Social Cognition* 8 (1): 1–8.

Lang, Annie. 1991. "Emotion, Formal Features, and Memory for Televised Political Advertisements." In Frank Biocca, ed., *Television and Political Advertising*. Vol. 1, pp. 221–44. Hillsdale, N.J.: Lawrence Erlbaum.

Larson, Stephanie Greco. 1990. "Information and Learning in a Congressional District: Social Experiment." *American Journal of Political Science* 34 (4): 1102–18.

Lau, Richard. 1982. "Negativity in Person Perception." *Political Behavior* 4 (4): 353–77.

———. 1985. "Two Explanations for Negativity Effects in Political Behavior." *American Journal of Political Science* 29 (1): 119–38.

Luntz, Frank I. 1988. *Candidates, Consultants, and Campaigns: The Style and Substance of American Electioneering*. Oxford: Basil Blackwell.

Mann, Thomas, and Raymond Wolfinger. 1980. "Candidates and Parties in Congressional Elections." *American Political Science Review* 74 (3): 617–32.

Martínez, Michael D., and Tad Delegal. 1990. "The Irrelevance of Negative Campaigns to Political Trust: Experimental and Survey Results." *Political Communication and Persuasion* 7 (January/March): 25–40.

McGraw, Kathleen M., and Marco Steenbergen. 1997. "Pictures in the Head: Memory Representation of Political Candidates." In Milton Lodge and Kathleen M. McGraw, eds., *Political Judgment: Structure and Process*. University of Michigan Press.

McLeod, Jack M., and Daniel McDonald. 1985. "Beyond Simple Exposure: Media Orientations and Their Impact on Political Processes." *Communication Research* 12 (1): 3–34.

Miller, Warren E., and J. Merrill Shanks. 1996. *The New American Voter.* Harvard University Press.

Newhagen, John E., and Byron Reeves. 1991. "Emotion and Memory Responses for Negative Political Advertising: A Study of Television Commercials Used in the 1988 Presidential Election." In Frank Biocca, ed., *Television and Political Advertising,* vol. 1, pp. 197–220. Hillsdale, N.J.: Lawrence Erlbaum.

Richey, Marjorie H., Frank S. Bono, Helen V. Lewis, and Harold W. Richey. 1982. "Selectivity of Negative Bias in Impression Formation." *Journal of Social Psychology* 116 (1): 107–18.

Robinson, Michael J., and Dennis K. Davis. 1990. "Television News and the Informed Public." *Journal of Communication* 40 (1): 106–19.

Rosenstone, Steven J., and John Mark Hansen. 1993. *Mobilization, Participation, and Democracy in America.* Macmillan.

Salmore, Barbara G., and Stephen A. Salmore. 1989. *Candidates, Parties, and Campaigns: Electoral Politics in America,* 2d ed. Washington, D.C.: Congressional Quarterly Press.

Squire, Peverill. 1989. "Challengers in U.S. Senate Elections." *Legislative Studies Quarterly* 14 (4): 531–47.

———. 1992. "Challenger Quality and Voting Behavior in U.S. Senate Elections." *Legislative Studies Quarterly* 17 (2): 247–64.

Westlye, Mark C. 1991. *Senate Elections and Campaign Intensity.* Johns Hopkins University Press.

Zaller, John R. 1992. *Nature and Origins of Mass Opinion.* Cambridge University Press.

Zhao, Xinshu, and Seven H. Chaffee. 1995. "Campaign Advertisements versus Television News as Sources of Political Issue Information." *Public Opinion Quarterly* 59 (1): 41–65.

CHAPTER FIVE

Agenda Setting and Campaign Advertising in Congressional Elections

PAUL S. HERRNSON

KELLY D. PATTERSON

DURING THE 1998 congressional elections, most Democratic candidates based their campaigns on protecting the environment and ensuring citizen access to affordable health care. Their Republican opponents ran on campaign platforms that focused on introducing new tax cuts and putting criminals behind bars. Candidates of both parties discussed improving education, saving social security, and a variety of other issues. Political advertising through television, radio, and direct mail was the key vehicle candidates used to deliver their messages to potential voters. The candidates recognized that using political advertising to set the campaign agenda would be a key element to achieving electoral success.

Issues are important in election campaigns. From the perspective of democratic theory, it matters a great deal that voters have the opportunity to learn about where candidates stand on issues. Ideally, campaigns inform citizens, offer them clear and distinct policy choices, and motivate them to participate in elections. Political advertising plays a key role in explaining policy choices to voters. Then voters respond to the information they receive from campaigns and cast their ballots for the candidate who most directly addresses their concerns.[1]

Yet it is clear that not all campaigns are equipped to influence the issues

We would like to thank Peter Francia and Carter Swift for their research assistance on this paper.
1. Dewey (1954 [1927]), p. 122.

that voters consider when casting their ballot. House races frequently pit entrenched, popular, well-funded incumbents against inexperienced, largely invisible, underfunded challengers.[2] Incumbents typically dominate the campaign agenda. They saturate the media with image-laden ads that focus on their personal characteristics, performance in office, or valence issues.[3] Challengers—most of whom are short on cash and campaign expertise, lack the resources to run a full-blown media campaign, and are unable to attract much free media—often struggle unsuccessfully to gain visibility among voters. In the few contests where an experienced or "quality" challenger emerges and is able to mount a credible campaign, incumbent spending increases, and incumbents focus more on issues, including the position or "wedge" issues that their opponents introduce into the campaign. Control over the campaign agenda is often up for grabs in these contests, and these elections become competitive.

Open-seat contests, which are often highly competitive, are among the most expensive and issue-oriented. Approximately 64 percent of all candidates in these contests make issues the primary focus of their campaign advertising.[4] The competitiveness of these elections is reflected in the battles the candidates wage to control the campaign agenda.

What impact do House campaigns have on how voters cast their ballots? With the exception of some experimental studies, the academic literature has largely ignored this question, focusing instead on voting behavior and the impact of national conditions on congressional elections.[5] In this chapter we assess the impact of House candidates' campaign communications and agenda-setting efforts on voters using a unique data set that combines information about House candidates' campaign platforms with information about voters' issue priorities and voting decisions.

When and Why Campaigns Matter

Three general types of explanations account for the choices that voters make during congressional campaigns: behavioral, structural, and strategic. Behavioral explanations generally emphasize voters' individual-level characteristics. Early studies of voting behavior tended to focus on group

2. Jacobson (1980), pp. 105–34.
3. Herrnson (1998), ch. 8 and 9.
4. Herrnson (1998), pp. 171–72.
5. Ansolabehere and Iyengar (1994); Ansolabehere, Behr, and Iyengar (1994).

characteristics, such as religion and ethnicity, which, it was argued, accounted for individuals' response to campaigns and their vote choices.[6] Later explanations concentrated on the importance of partisanship. They considered party identification, defined as a lasting attachment to one of the major political parties, as an exogenous predictor of vote choice that varied little over time.[7] Other individual-level variables, such as gender, age, and education, also were believed to influence voting behavior. A common element that united the early literature was that voting decisions were considered relatively impervious to election campaigns. Campaigns normally were viewed as having no impact or, at most, as activating the partisan attachments that would then determine the voter's choice.[8]

Recent behavioral research has demonstrated that factors other than party identification and demographic characteristics can influence election outcomes, indicating that personal skills and motivations can influence an individual's awareness of and responsiveness to political campaigns. Party identification, which traditionally has been viewed as a stable attitude, can change in response to campaigns and the issues staked out by candidates.[9] Campaigns can have an impact on congressional voters under some circumstances.

Voters with high levels of political awareness are likely to react to campaigns that receive intense media coverage. These individuals also tend to be more informed about low-intensity elections than their less-informed counterparts.[10] Voters who care little about politics are less likely to know much about elections, but they are more likely to change their partisan or issue preferences if exposed to information in a campaign.[11] However, because these individuals have low levels of political awareness, they are unlikely to receive campaign communications that could influence their opinions, and they rarely get beyond learning about the candidate's persona and, at most, a few issues.[12] Campaigns that receive intense media scrutiny, however, can have an effect on these voters.[13]

Structural explanations often focus on the conditions surrounding the race, such as whether an incumbent is seeking reelection, the geographic

6. Berelson, Lazarsfeld, and McPhee (1954).
7. Campbell and others (1960), p. 64.
8. Finkel (1993).
9. Box-Steffensmeier and Smith (1996). See also MacKuen (1984).
10. See Zaller (1992); see also Bartels (1986).
11. Converse (1962), p. 579.
12. Zaller (1992, 1993); McGuire (1998); Brians and Wattenberg (1996).
13. Zaller (1993), p. 377.

and partisan characteristics of the district, and the nature of its media market. Incumbent-challenger campaigns are usually less competitive and tend to draw less media coverage than open-seat contests. Because the media provide citizens with less election-related information about incumbent-challenger elections, these campaigns have less of an impact on individuals' voting decisions.

Money also has an impact on House elections. Campaigns that spend large sums are better able to reach voters and influence their vote.[14] These campaigns generally have more money to spend on political advertising and typically spend two-thirds of their campaign budgets on paid media. These campaigns also have a greater potential to influence the votes of less educated and less politically aware individuals. Campaign spending by challengers and open-seat candidates is especially important.[15]

Strategic explanations focus on the decisions that candidates make when they wage their campaigns. Candidates' strategies are designed to maximize their opportunity to win. Candidates adopt some issue positions out of conviction but select many others for strategic reasons. Providing voters with complete information about the issues is not a relevant consideration for most campaigns. Rather, giving blocs of swing voters a reason to support the candidates is a major goal of those who plan and wage campaigns.

The campaign strategies that candidates adopt can have a significant effect on the clarity of voter perceptions. Candidates who vacillate on policy positions or focus on just one or two highly charged symbolic issues may attract voter support, despite the fact that their campaigns rarely provide voters with complete information on the major issues. In some cases, campaigns may do more to confuse voters than to educate them. For example, when candidates focus on exploiting their opponent's weaknesses, voters typically are less able to distinguish between the two contenders.[16]

The techniques that candidates use to communicate their messages afford little opportunity to present a detailed discussion of the issues. Television ads, which nearly half of all voters cite as their most important source of information on House candidates, are better suited to setting an agenda and conveying images than to presenting policy alternatives.[17] Radio ads

14. Kenny and McBurnett (1994).
15. Jacobson (1980, 1990); Herrnson (1998), pp. 206–13. For another point of view, see Green and Krasno (1988, 1990).
16. Franklin (1991).
17. See Patterson (1993). See also West (1993), especially chapter 4.

are just as useful as television for conveying emotion-laden messages and almost as poor at presenting detailed discussions of complex issues.[18]

Negative campaigning also discourages meaningful policy discussions. Attack ads, name calling, and other forms of mudslinging have become commonplace in congressional elections. These are used more frequently in competitive than in noncompetitive elections.[19] The overall effect of negative campaigning discourages voters, alienating them from the political process.[20]

Many candidates attempt to become associated with "valence" issues such as a strong economy, job creation, domestic tranquillity, and international security because they generate widespread support while creating little opposition.[21] The median voter theory states that candidates in homogeneous districts tend to take the same stands on major issues because electoral imperatives encourage both Democrats and Republicans to adopt policy positions that appeal to the vast majority of voters.[22] However, not all districts are homogeneous, and not all campaigns focus on valence issues. Some candidates use ads to set a political agenda that is based on "position" or "wedge" issues they believe to be advantageous to their cause.[23] Democratic candidates recognize that members of their party usually do well when the campaign agenda focuses on education, health care, or the environment. Republicans recognize that their standard-bearers are most successful when voters focus on cutting taxes, fighting crime, and reducing the size of government.

Some campaigns work to set an election agenda that focuses on position issues that are likely to prove beneficial to their candidate. Three campaigns waged in North Carolina's fourth district illustrate the importance of setting the issue agenda in House races. In the 1992 House race, Representative David Price sought to focus the election on education and worker training, which he labeled the two keys to the nation's economic recovery.[24] These issues were intended to attract the support of blue-collar workers, an important group of swing voters in his district. His unsuccessful opponent, Republican challenger La Vinia "Vicky" Goudie, ran ads

18. Luntz (1988), p. 108.
19. Herrnson (1998), pp. 177–80; Skaperdas and Grofman (1995).
20. Ansolabehere and others (1994); Kahn and Kenney in chapter 4 of this volume.
21. Stokes (1966).
22. See Fiorina (1974). See also Stokes (1966); Downs (1957), pp. 111-113.
23. Herrnson (1998), pp. 172–174.
24. Herrnson (1998), p. 173.

focused on Price's bounced checks and the need for government reform.[25] Price spent thirty-seven times more than Goudie, enabling him to dominate the campaign agenda, and the airwaves, and to win by a 31 percent vote margin.

Two years later, Price was defeated by Republican challenger Fred Heineman, a former police chief. Heineman ran ads that focused the election on crime, drug abuse, and corruption in Washington. His antigovernment, anticrime message paralleled the themes in the House Republicans' Contract with America. A campaign war chest of $278,000—about 40 percent of Price's total receipts—and a national campaign agenda that favored Republicans resulted in Heineman becoming a member of the U.S. House of Representatives' historic Republican class of 1994.

Two years after Price was defeated, he challenged Heineman to a rematch. This time, Price's platform of education, economic fairness, and Republican proposals to reduce funding for medicare and social security were central issues on the national agenda. Price used these issues to win the support of swing voters. He also ran ads attacking his opponent for being out of touch with the district. Heineman tried to focus the election agenda on the same crime-related antigovernment issues that helped him wrest the seat away from Price in the watershed election of 1994. Although spending in the race was relatively even, Price was able to set the campaign agenda in 1996 and won by a 10 percent vote margin.[26] The candidates' ability to use political advertising to influence the campaign agenda had a major effect on the outcome of these elections.

Data and Methodology

Campaign agendas and issues probably have been important in many campaigns for Congress, but researchers should be skeptical about claims based on a few case studies such as those we have described here. This study is unique in that it uses a representative data set to assess systematically the impact of congressional campaign agendas on voting behavior.[27] The data

25. Interview with Richard Goudie, campaign manager, Vicky Goudie for Congress Committee, April 18, 1994.

26. Herrnson (1998), pp. 172–73, 186.

27. The Voter Research Survey and the campaign survey provide representative samples of the underlying populations of interest: voters in House districts and House candidates. When the two samples were combined and analyzed in the multivariate models, some cases were lost due to missing data. Nevertheless, the resulting sample was representative of both

set includes both the issues that the candidates reported were most important in their election and the issues that voters identified as being most
important to their voting decision.[28] It enables us to analyze how issue
agreement affects the way individuals vote in congressional elections.

We posit that issue agreement is largely the result of the strategic decisions reached by candidates and their campaign aides. This assumption
contrasts with what political skeptics believe about the use of research
tools such as public opinion polls and focus groups. Skeptics hold that
candidates select their issues only after consulting polls and focus groups.
In their view, issue agreement between candidates and voters is poll-driven
and artificially created rather than the result of the agenda-setting efforts
of candidates.

We reject the skeptics' assumption for several reasons. First, most House
candidates are drawn to politics because they care deeply about some issues, and candidates are unlikely to ignore those issues when they campaign for Congress. Second, all incumbents and all nonincumbents with
office-holding experience possess political records. Most House candidates
are proud of their accomplishments and seek to discuss them. They also
recognize that they cannot ignore those aspects of their records that could
become political liabilities. Thus candidates seek to set an agenda that
presents them in a favorable light, instead of allowing their opponent or
the media to set the agenda. Finally, we recognize that many candidates
take polls to learn about public concerns and to ascertain how voters are
likely to react to different messages, but for the reasons stated above they

---

the universe of congressional election campaigns and the universe of congressional voters
(see tables 5A-1 and 5A-2). For more information on the surveys, see Herrnson (1998), pp.
262–71; Institute for Social Research (1995–96), p. 143.

28. The variables for issue agreement were created by matching candidate and voter
responses to questions about the most important issue in the congressional campaign. The
candidates were asked, "What do you think were the most important issues in your campaign? (You may list local and/or national issues)." Most candidates listed one issue, some
listed two, and a few listed three. The exit poll asked, "Which one or two issues mattered
most in deciding how you voted? Health care, federal budget deficit, abortion, education,
economy/jobs, environment, taxes, foreign policy, family values." We coded voters and
candidates as being in agreement on the issues whenever they agreed on at least one issue.
Voters who agreed with one or more of the Democratic candidate's issue priorities, but
none of the Republican's priorities, were coded as agreeing with the Democrat. Voters who
agreed with one or more of the Republican candidate's issue priorities, but none of the
Democrat's priorities, were coded as agreeing with the Republican. Voters who agreed with
at least one of the issue priorities of each candidate were coded as agreeing with both. The
remainder of the voters were coded as agreeing with neither candidate.

are unlikely to try to run away from their records in an attempt to please voters. Moreover, when candidates respond to what they learn in public opinion polls by emphasizing one aspect of their record and downplaying others, it is the candidates, not the voters, who are responsible for this decision. And, it is the candidates, not the voters, who have set the campaign agenda. The candidates could just as easily have chosen to stress other issues, thereby resulting in a different set of issues forming the campaign agenda.

This study combines data from two different sources. The first is the Voter Research Surveys and General Election Exit Poll in 1992. The Voter Research Surveys polled more than 15,000 voters in the fifty states. The precinct was the sampling unit, but the poll included a code to match respondents with their congressional district.[29] The exit poll contained information about the respondents' issue positions, party identification, and voting behavior.

The second source of data is a survey of congressional campaigns that used a mail questionnaire to collect information about campaign strategy, issues, advertising, expenditures on campaign communications, and other important aspects of congressional elections. The questionnaire was mailed to all major-party candidates and campaign aides who competed in the 1992 congressional elections. The survey had a response rate of 42 percent, and the sample closely approximates the population of interest on key variables such as party affiliation, incumbency, and election outcome.[30]

The two data sets were merged so that we could match the policy positions of the congressional candidates with those of the voters who reside in their district. The resulting data set has information about congressional candidates' campaigns, voters' political dispositions and voting behavior, and the issues that both candidates and voters in their district identified as being the most important in the election. It contains information from thirty congressional districts and 694 congressional voters. The sample is representative of the universe of congressional districts, except that it includes slightly more open seats and marginal districts. It also is representative of the universe of congressional voters.[31]

---

29. These codes were not available in the Institute for Social Research (1995–96) version of the data, but the Voter Research Survey released the codes to the authors so respondents could be matched with their congressional districts. For the complete description of the data set, see the Institute for Social Research (1992), p. 413.

30. For a detailed discussion of the survey, see the appendix in Herrnson (1998).

31. For more information on the sample, see tables 5A-1 and 5A-2 in the appendix.

Unlike traditional data sets that have sought to measure the relationship between national campaigns and national public opinion, this data set has an ample number of cases in each congressional district to make multivariate analysis across many districts possible. Unfortunately, the data set has two shortcomings. First, party identification, a key explanatory variable, is crudely measured, and this introduces some difficulties into our analysis. Second, the data set does not contain a measure of exposure to campaign advertising. However, survey measures of exposure to mass advertising are not very reliable.[32] We assume that, because our data set relies on voters rather than on registered or likely voters, individuals already have demonstrated more interest in politics and more likely have followed at least part of the campaigns. Furthermore, unlike most experimental designs, an exit poll has the luxury of measuring vote choice instead of probable vote choice. Following a preliminary examination of the data, we used cross-tabulations to assess the impact that shared issue priorities have on how voters cast their congressional votes.

Congressional Campaigns and Voting Decisions

Do voters respond to the campaigns waged by congressional candidates?[33] The evidence presented in table 5-1 provides a preliminary indication that they do. Candidates and voters focused on five major issues during the 1992 congressional elections. The economy was clearly the number one concern of both groups. More than three-quarters of all candidates rated it as one of the most important items on their campaign agenda. Approximately 75 percent of all Democratic voters, 53 percent of all Republican voters, and 68 percent of all independent voters also rated it as one of the most important issues in the election.

The second most important issue in the election for Democratic candidates was health care reform, whereas Republican candidates focused on the federal budget deficit, and voters were concerned with taxes. Nevertheless, candidate and voter issue priorities were not very different on

32. See Ansolabehere and others (1994), p. 830.
33. This chapter does not rely on a measure of the campaign advertising used by congressional candidates. We assume that what most candidates thought was the most important issue in the campaign was also the subject of much of their campaign communications. In a subsequent survey of congressional candidates in the 1998 campaign, we find that there is a high correlation between what candidates think is the most important issue in a campaign and what subjects are the focus of their campaign advertising. These data are available from the authors.

Table 5-1. *The Most Important Issues Identified by Candidates and Voters in the 1992 House Elections*
Percent unless otherwise noted

	Candidates		Voters		
Issue	Democrats	Republicans	Democrats	Republicans	Indepen-dents
Economy	76.7	76.7	75.1	52.6	68.1
Federal budget deficit	10.0	23.3	19.2	27.0	31.6
Health care reform	23.3	13.3	35.9	24.2	23.5
Abortion	13.3	3.3	15.4	17.0	16.1
Taxes	6.7	3.3	48.3	42.8	49.3
Number	30	30	256	265	173

Source: The candidate data are from the 1992 Congressional Campaign Study; see Herrnson (1995), app., and the voter data are from Institute for Social Research (1995–96). Cell entries are for the percentage of candidates or voters who identified the issue as the two or three most important issues in the election. The analysis includes only issues included in both questionnaires, which eliminated a small number of candidate responses that referred to foreign policy, social issues, and some candidate-related issues. Columns do not sum to 100 because many respondents designated more than one issue as important.

these issues: the Democratic voters' third most important election priority was health care reform, and Republican voters' third ranked priority was the budget deficit. Finally, abortion was a major campaign issue for only about 13 percent of all Democratic candidates, 3 percent of all Republican candidates, and approximately 16 percent of all voters. Candidates and voters were clearly attuned to the same policy concerns during the 1992 congressional elections.

More than half of the electorate shared the issue priorities of one or both of the candidates running in their congressional district (see table 5-2). Approximately 13 percent of all voters shared only the Democratic candidate's issue priorities, and about 11 percent shared only the Republican candidate's priorities. About 35 percent of all voters shared some of the major issue concerns of each candidate. Slightly more than 40 percent of all voters were unaware of or did not agree with either the Democratic or Republican candidate's major platform issues. This lack of agreement is due at least in part to the general public's low level of issue awareness in congressional elections.

Most voters use their party identification as a perceptual screen that encourages them to pay attention to and remember the campaign activities of their party's candidates and to ignore those of the opposition.[34]

34. Campbell and others (1960), p. 102.

Table 5-2. *The Frequency of Candidate and Voter Agreement on the Most Important Issues in the 1992 House Elections*
Percent unless otherwise noted

Candidates	All voters	Democratic voters	Republican voters	Independent voters
Democrats	13.0	17.2	10.2	11.0
Republicans	11.1	10.5	11.7	11.0
Both	35.0	37.1	28.3	42.0
No agreement	40.9	35.2	49.8	35.8
Number	694	256	265	173

Source: The candidate data are from the 1992 Congressional Campaign Study; see Herrnson (1995), app., and the voter data are from Institute for Social Research (1995–96). Cell entries are for the percentage of candidates or voters who identified the issue as the two or three most important issues in the election. The analysis includes only issues included in both questionnaires, which eliminated a small number of candidate responses that referred to foreign policy, social issues, and some candidate-related issues. Columns do not sum to 100 because many respondents designated more than one issue as important. Some columns do not add to 100 percent due to rounding.
$\chi^2 = 20.1$.
$p < 0.01$.

This is visible through their responsiveness to the communications of their party's candidate. About 17 percent of all Democratic voters agreed with the issue priorities that formed the unique portion of their Democratic candidate's campaign agenda. By contrast, only 10 percent of all Republicans and 11 percent of all independents shared those priorities. Slightly more Republican than Democratic and independent voters agreed with the Republican candidate's issue priorities. The level of issue agreement between Democratic candidates and Democratic voters is significantly higher than that between Republican candidates and Republican voters, indicating that the Democrats had somewhat greater success in setting the campaign agenda.

The Democrats' agenda-setting advantages in 1992 can be attributed partially to the fact that more Democratic than Republican incumbents were seeking reelection. Incumbents' spending advantages help many of them to set the campaign agenda. The dovetailing of many Democratic House candidates' issue priorities with those of the party's popular presidential candidate, Bill Clinton, probably also helped the Democrats to attract support for their campaign platforms from voters in their district. Nevertheless, it is important not to overstate the Democrats' advantage in setting the agenda. More than 40 percent of all independents shared issue priorities with both the Democratic and the Republican candidate. Independents constitute an important group of swing voters. Their voting de-

Table 5-3. *The Impact of Issue Agreement on Congressional Voting Decisions*
Percent

	Issue agreement with				
Vote for	Democratic candidate	Republican candidate	Both candidates	Neither candidate	Number
Democrat	62.3	55.8	62.6	42.3	323
Republican	37.8	44.2	37.4	57.7	371

Source: The candidate data are from the 1992 Congressional Campaign Study; see Herrnson (1995), app., and the voter data are from Institute for Social Research (1995–96). Cell entries are for the percentage of candidates or voters who identified the issue as the two or three most important issues in the election. The analysis includes only issues included in both questionnaires, which eliminated a small number of candidate responses that referred to foreign policy, social issues, and some candidate-related issues. Columns do not sum to 100 because many respondents designated more than one issue as important. Some columns do not add to 100 percent due to rounding.
$\chi^2 = 17.0$.
$p < 0.001$.
$N = 694$.

cisions can often determine which candidate emerges victorious on election day.

Of course, campaign agenda setting is only a means to an end. Attracting voter support is a campaign's major goal. Voters who share issue priorities with one but not both candidates in their congressional district should exhibit greater support for the candidate they agree with than for the other. More than 62 percent of all congressional voters who agreed with the Democratic candidate (but not the Republican) voted for the Democrat in the 1992 elections (see table 5-3). However, this expectation was not borne out for issue agreement with the Republican candidate: 56 percent of all voters who agreed with the Republican contestant voted for the Democrat. Two other findings reported in the table are that voters who agree with at least one of each candidate's issue priorities are most likely to vote for the Democrat, and voters who agree with neither candidate's issue priorities are most likely to vote for the Republican. These findings suggest that other factors, besides issue agreement, influence how voters cast their congressional ballot.

Party identification has an important impact on individuals' awareness of, interest in, and attitudes toward politics. It has a major effect on individuals' voting decisions. More than 93 percent of all Democratic voters who agree with the issue priorities of their party's candidate vote for that candidate (see table 5-4). Roughly the same number of Democrats who agree with the Republican candidate's issue priorities also vote for the

Table 5-4. *The Impact of Issue Agreement on Congressional Voting Decisions Controlling for Party Identification*
Percent

	Issue agreement with			
Voters	Democratic candidate	Republican candidate	Both candidates	Neither candidate
Democratic voters				
Democrat	93.2	92.6	90.5	85.6
Republican	6.8	7.4	9.5	19.4
Republican voters				
Democrat	25.9	19.4	22.7	9.1
Republican	74.1	80.6	77.3	90.9
Independent voters				
Democrat	42.1	63.2	67.1	50.0
Republican	57.9	36.8	32.9	50.0

Source: The candidate data are from the 1992 Congressional Campaign Study; see Herrnson (1995), app., and the voter data are from Institute for Social Research (1995–96). Cell entries are for the percentage of candidates or voters who identified the issue as the two or three most important issues in the election. The analysis includes only issues included in both questionnaires, which eliminated a small number of candidate responses that referred to foreign policy, social issues, and some candidate-related issues. Columns do not sum to 100 because many respondents designated more than one issue as important. The wording of the questions appears in the appendix.
$\chi^2 = 12.9$.
$p < 0.01$.
$N = 694$.

Democratic candidate. Fewer Democrats who agree with some of each candidate's issue priorities or who share issue priorities with neither candidate vote for the Democrat, but the percentages are still above 85 percent. Party identification has an overwhelming impact on Democrats' congressional voting decisions. Shared issue concerns have an important reinforcing effect on most Democratic voters.

Republican voters also are heavily influenced by partisanship, but issue agreement has a greater influence on how they cast their congressional ballots. Approximately one-quarter of all Republican voters who share the Democratic candidate's issue priorities (but not the Republican's) defect to support the Democrat. More than one-fifth of all voters who share some of each candidate's issue priorities defect to the Democrat. As one would expect, voters who share the Republican candidate's major issue concerns are among the least likely to defect. Only voters who agree with neither candidate's issue platforms are more loyal.

Independent voters are influenced by candidates' agenda-setting efforts, but not in ways that one would expect. Independents who agree with the Democratic candidate's issue priorities are more likely to vote for the Republican than for the Democrat, and those who agree with the Republican candidate's issue priorities are more likely to vote for the Democrat. Independents who agree with neither candidate's stand on issues are equally likely to vote for either candidate, whereas most of those who are informed about both candidates' issue priorities vote for the Democrat. There seem to be two reasons for these counterintuitive results. First, they may reflect the tendency of some independent voters to exhibit less interest in politics and campaigns. Second, the measurement of partisanship used by the Voter Research Surveys lumps all partisans together. It does not distinguish between independents who lean toward either the Republican or the Democratic party. However, previous research has shown that some independents act in a more partisan manner than individuals who first identify with one of the major parties.[35] The inclusion of partisans and independents into the one category may confound some of the results for independents.

Conclusions

This chapter shows that campaigns can influence how citizens vote in congressional elections. It demonstrates that most voters cast their ballot for candidates who share their issue priorities. Under most circumstances, issue congruence reinforces voters' partisan dispositions, but it also can encourage citizens to cross party lines when casting their congressional ballot.

Studies that examine the impact of political dispositions and demographic traits on voting behavior do not fully capture the dynamics of congressional elections. Elections involve the interplay of issues, campaign strategies, and voter attitudes. Candidates use political advertising, among other techniques, to attempt to set a partisan campaign agenda that works to their advantage. The campaign agenda, in turn, interacts with voters' disposition to influence how they cast their ballot. A full explanation of the dynamics of congressional elections must examine campaign communications, including political advertising, to fully understand candidates' agenda-setting efforts.

35. See Keith and others (1992), ch. 4 and 5.

Table 5A-1. *Indicators of the Representativeness of the Congressional Districts in the Sample*
Percent

Indicator	Sample[a]	Population[a]
Seat status		
Open	73	77
Incumbent-occupied	27	23
District competitiveness		
Marginal	47	41
Uncompetitive	53	59

a. Contested districts only.

Table 5A-2. *Indicators of the Representativeness of the Congressional Voters in the Sample*
Percent

Indicator	Sample[a]	Population[a]
Age		
25–29	10	6
30–39	28	10
40–49	26	26
50–64	19	19
65 and older	9	18
Sex		
Male	49	47
Female	51	53
Education		
Did not complete high school	4	11
High school graduate	22	30
Some college, but no degree	30	26
College graduate	27	14
Postgraduate study	16	13
Partisanship		
Democrat	37	37
Republican	38	28
Minor party	2	0.2
Independent	23	35

Source: Population data are from the 1992 National Election Study enhanced file.
a. Congressional voters only. Some columns do not add to 100 percent due to rounding.

References

Ansolabehere, Stephen, Roy Behr, and Shanto Iyengar. 1994. *Media Game: American Politics in the Television Age.* Macmillan.

Ansolabehere, Stephen, and Shanto Iyengar. 1994. "Joint Effects of Advertising and News Coverage in Campaigns." *Public Opinion Quarterly* 58 (3): 335–57.

Ansolabhere, Stephen, Shanto Iyengar, Adam Simon, and Nicholas Valentino. 1994. "Does Attack Advertising Demobilize the Electorate?" *American Political Science Review* 88 (December): 829–38.

Bartels, Larry M. 1986. "Issue Voting under Uncertainty: An Empirical Test." *American Journal of Political Science* 30 (4): 709–28.

Berelson, Bernard R., Paul F. Lazarsfeld, and William McPhee. 1954. *Voting: A Study of Opinion Formation in a Presidential Campaign.* University of Chicago Press.

Box-Steffensmeier, Janet M., and Renee M. Smith. 1996. "The Dynamics of Aggregate Partisanship." *American Political Science Review* 90 (3): 567–80.

Brians, Craig Leonard, and Martin P. Wattenberg. 1996. "Campaign Issue Knowledge and Salience: Comparing Reception from TV Commercials, TV News, and Newspapers." *American Journal of Political Science* 40 (1): 172–93.

Campbell, Angus, Philip E. Converse, Warren E. Miller, and Donald E. Stokes. 1960. *The American Voter.* John Wiley and Sons.

Converse, Philip E. 1962. "The Nature of Belief Systems in Mass Publics." In David Apter, ed., *Ideology and Discontent.* Free Press.

Dewey, John. 1954 [1927]. *The Public and Its Problems.* Athens, Ohio: Swallow Press.

Downs, Anthony. 1957. *An Economic Theory of Democracy.* Harper Collins.

Finkel, Steven. 1993. "Reexamining the 'Minimal Effect' Model in Recent Presidential Campaigns." *Journal of Politics* 55 (1): 1–21.

Fiorina, Morris P. 1974. *Congress: Keystone of the Washington Establishment.* Yale University Press.

Franklin, Charles H. 1991. "Eschewing Obfuscation? Campaigns and the Perception of U.S. Senate Incumbents." *American Political Science Review* 85 (4): 1193–214.

Green, Donald P., and Jonathan S. Krasno. 1988. "Salvation for the Spendthrift Incumbent: Reestimating the Effects of Campaign Spending in House Elections." *American Journal of Political Science* 32 (4): 884–907.

———. 1990. "Rebuttal to Jacobson's 'New Evidence for Old Arguments.'" *American Journal of Political Science* 34 (2): 363–72.

Herrnson, Paul S. 1995. *Congressional Elections: Campaigning at Home and in Washington,* 1st ed. Washington, D.C.: Congressional Quarterly Press.

———. 1998. *Congressional Elections: Campaigning at Home and in Washington,* 2d ed. Washington, D.C.: Congressional Quarterly Press.

Institute for Social Research. 1992. *Voter Research and Surveys General Election Exit Polls, 1992.* University of Michigan, Institute for Social Research.

———. 1995–96. *ICPSR Guide to Resources and Services, Voter Research and Surveys General Election Exit Polls, 1992.* University of Michigan, Institute for Social Research.

Jacobson, Gary C. 1980. *Money in Congressional Elections.* Yale University Press.
————. 1990. "The Effects of Congressional Campaigning in House Elections: New Evidence for Old Arguments." *American Journal of Political Science* 34 (2): 334–62.
Keith, Bruce E., David B. Magleby, Candice J. Nelson, Elizabeth Orr, Mark C. Westlye, and Raymond E. Wolfinger. 1992. *The Myth of the Independent Voter.* University of California Press.
Kenny, Christopher, and Michael McBurnett. 1994. "An Individual-Level Multiequation Model of Expenditure Effects in Contested House Elections." *American Political Science Review* 88 (3): 699–707.
Luntz, Frank I. 1988. *Candidates, Consultants, and Campaigns.* Oxford: Basil Blackwell.
MacKuen, Michael. 1984. "Exposure to Information, Belief Integration, and Individual Responsiveness to Agenda Change." *American Political Science Review* 78 (2): 372–91.
McGuire, William. 1998. "The Nature of Attitudes and Attitude Change." In Gardner Lindzey and Elliot Aronson, eds., *Handbook of Social Psychology.* Vol. 2. Addison-Wesley.
Patterson, Thomas E. 1993. *Out of Order.* Knopf.
Skaperdas, Stergios, and Bernard Grofman. 1995. "Modeling Negative Campaigning." *American Political Science Review* 89 (1): 49–61.
Stokes, Donald F. 1966. "Some Dynamic Elements of Contests for the Presidency." *American Political Science Review* 69 (3): 812–26.
West, Darrell M. 1993. *Air Wars: Television Advertising in Election Campaigns, 1952–1992.* Washington, D.C.: Congressional Quarterly Press.
Zaller, John R. 1992. *The Nature and Origins of Mass Opinion.* Cambridge, U.K.: Cambridge University Press.
————. 1993. "The Converse-McGuire Model of Attitude Change and the Gulf War Opinion Rally." *Political Communication* 10 (4): 369–88.

CHAPTER SIX

"Basic Rule" Voting: Impact of Campaigns on Party- and Approval-Based Voting

SHANTO IYENGAR
JOHN R. PETROCIK

AMERICAN POLITICS HAS A "fifth estate" of campaign managers and political consultants who are believed to be able to design campaign strategies and tactics that persuade voters to support their candidate.[1] This conventional wisdom makes their services almost essential for many campaigns, and the credibility of a candidate's effort often is judged by the reputation and win-loss record (and sometimes they are equivalent) of the consultants working for the campaign. The use of consultants is so widespread that it is not difficult to find jurisdictions where political operatives (albeit minor ones) are plying their trade near the bottom of the ballot in races for school boards, municipal judgeships, and county commissions. The sine qua non of their prominence is a prior belief that campaigns shape the outcome of elections. How much consultants contribute to the efficacy of a campaign is a subject of debate and not one that we will attempt to resolve.[2] This chapter addresses the efficacy of campaigns themselves.

There is evidence of campaign effects. "Attack" campaigning, canvassing, voter contact, party organization work, campaign spending, media coverage, candidate appearances, television advertising, and the activities of political consultants have been studied for their effects on turnout, can-

---

1. See the interesting exchange on the 1980 election between Pat Caddell (1981) and Richard Wirthlin (1981), major advisers to, respectively, Jimmy Carter and Ronald Reagan; see also Bradshaw (1995) and Thurber and Nelson (2000).
2. For studies that do address this question, see Herrnson (2000) and Medvic (2000).

didate images, fundraising, and election outcomes.[3] This work has not, however, produced anything near a consensus that campaigns are as important as one would expect given the money and attention lavished on them.

There is a strong correlation between the vote and structural variables (a term used here as a shorthand for national economic conditions, incumbent approval, domestic and foreign tranquility, the honesty and integrity of officials, and standing predispositions, such as party identification). This correlation has persuaded many political scientists (few of whom, it must be admitted, have any experience in campaigns) that election outcomes are shaped by factors largely immune to campaign strategies and the maneuvering of candidates. Some findings—for example, that a president's *pre-campaign* popularity accounts for more than two-thirds of the variance of the vote of the incumbent party—are especially severe blows to the notion that campaigns move the vote.[4] It is not surprising, therefore, that forecasting models based on structural indicators have been used extensively to predict election results and that none has incorporated campaign-specific strategies, tactics, or events. Their predictive success has shaped a dominant theory of retrospective voting that allows very little room for candidate maneuvering because the structural variables that candidates cannot manipulate are in place before a campaign begins.[5] In this theory, elections are referenda on the leadership of the incumbent president: voters pass judgment on the incumbent's overall record, but particularly on the economic performance of the current administration. Many general reviews and applications of these forecasting models have been done.[6] Corroborating individual-level studies have only reinforced the notion that campaigns have limited and maybe insignificant net effects.

3. On "attack" campaigning, see Pfau and Kensky (1990); Ansolabehere et al. (1994). On canvassing and voter contact, see Huckfeldt and Sprague (1992). On party organization work, see Herrnson (1988). On campaign spending, see Jacobson (1992). On media coverage, see Hershey (1989); Bartels (1993). On candidate appearances and television advertising, see Shaw (1999). And on the activities of political consultants, see Herrnson (1992, 2000); Medvic and Lenart (1997); Medvic (2000).

4. Hibbs (1987), ch. 6.

5. The theory of retrospective voting dates to at least V. O. Key's classic treatise *The Responsible Voter* (Key 1966), but also see Fiorina (1981).

6. See Abramowitz (1988, 1996); Lewis-Beck and Rice (1992); Alvarez and Nagler (1995); Markus (1988); Kinder (1997); Campbell and Mann (1992); Greene (1993); Brody and Sigelman (1983); Erikson (1989); Rosenstone (1983).

The near-conventional academic wisdom, therefore, is that day-to-day campaign events and tactics are mostly "sound and fury signifying nothing."[7] Even some of the most recent assessments indicate that campaigns have no net effect because each strategic move by a campaign is countered by its opponent.[8]

Explaining Weak Campaign Effects

Researchers have proposed a variety of theories to explain why campaign effects may be so limited.[9] One of the most prominent is the theory of offsetting effects, which accepts that campaigns can influence voters but that they almost always have a minimal net impact because the competitors neutralize each other because of a relative parity of resources, including both funding and know-how.[10]

A second set of explanations for minimal campaign effects asserts that their seeming irrelevance is actually illusory. This account focuses on methodological considerations, particularly the limitations of survey research. The founding fathers of campaign research (Paul Lazarsfeld and Bernard Berelson and their successors at the University of Michigan's Institute for Social Research) pioneered the use of sample surveys on the premise that survey respondents' self-reports are reliable and accurate and that the standard test of a campaign effect—the scale of differences in vote choice between respondents who self-report high or low levels of exposure to the campaign—accurately tests campaign effects.[11]

If self-reports are not accurate, then the absence of observable campaign effects can be attributed to measurement error. In most ways and at most times self-reports seem trustworthy, but there is good reason to believe that reports of campaign exposure are seriously erroneous, because the frailties of human memory create considerable slippage between what respondents say they saw or heard and what actually transpired. The avail-

---

7. See Markus (1988); Bartels (1992, 1997a); Gelman and King (1993).

8. Shaw (1999).

9. For a review of this literature, see Iyengar (1996).

10. See Markus (1988); Gelman and King (1993). One would expect that these conditions are satisfied for presidential campaigns, but not for most other campaigns.

11. The NES interview schedule, for instance, typically includes an extensive battery of questions concerning media exposure (frequency of television news viewing).

able evidence indicates that self-reported and actual exposure are only weakly correlated.[12]

Adding even further to the measurement error is the fact that self-reported exposure to campaign messages often is related to political attitudes, including candidate preference, because those who choose to tune in to the campaign may differ systematically (in ways that matter to their vote choice) from those who do not. Respondents who recalled seeing a campaign advertisement in the 1992 National Election Study (NES) survey, for instance, were more likely to intend to vote than those who did not.[13] Was it exposure to advertising that prompted turnout, or was the greater interest in campaigns among likely voters responsible for their higher level of recall? Most survey-based analyses of campaigns cannot disentangle the reciprocal effects of self-reported exposure and partisan attitudes.

Finally, a failure to observe campaign effects may reflect the short time frame during which most NES surveys (the most widely used survey data in academic circles) are collected. NES fieldwork begins around September 1—the traditional kickoff date for presidential campaigning. Fifty years ago the election might have been shaped significantly during the sixty or so days between September 1 and the election, but the modern system of "permanent" campaigns and months of highly visible campaigning before election day has created an environment in which most voters arrive at their choice of presidential candidate well before September 1. The small changes that occur after that date, even if they tip the balance, may be too small for surveys to detect.

Each of these hypotheses about the apparently limited effect of campaigns—offsetting effects, inadequate measurement of campaign exposure, and the time frame of the observations—is consistent with the observed facts. Our purpose in this chapter is not to choose among them, but to suggest that the "mystery of the irrelevant campaign" may be more apparent than real. The fact that partisanship and the popularity of the incumbent president are powerful determinants of voter choice is not inconsistent with the view that campaigns also influence these choices. Rather than treating structural and campaign-based accounts of elections as mutually exclusive, we see them as complementary.

---

12. Examples are provided in Price and Zaller (1993). In the experiments conducted by Ansolabehere and Iyengar (1995), for example, more than 50 percent of the participants who were exposed to a campaign advertisement were unable, a mere thirty minutes later, to recall having seen the advertisement.

13. Wattenberg and Brians (1996).

In this view, voters are guided by their party affiliation and their assessments of the performance of the incumbent exactly because exposure to the campaign serves to make these factors even more tightly bound up with candidate preferences. We suggest that, "Campaigns matter because they tend to produce congruence between fundamental political conditions and predispositions, on the one hand, and vote intentions, on the other."[14]

Campaigns as Activation

The analysis reported here provides evidence that campaigns shape the vote by activating underlying predispositions and perceptions. Considerable evidence from both the pre- and post-television eras suggests that presidential campaigns strengthen existing predispositions. The most basic predisposition, of course, is party identification, and exposure to the campaign tends to harden partisan loyalties, making it less likely that partisans will defect. This is not a new argument. The idea and evidence for it go back to the earliest voting studies, and contemporary survey studies provide considerable evidence that activation occurs as voters converge on the predictable choice, usually the candidate of the party preferred by the voter.

During the 1940 campaign Lazarsfeld and his collaborators found that many undecided voters converged on the "right" candidate: the one whose party was most closely associated with the voter's interests (measured indirectly through socioeconomic status, religion, and place of residence).[15] Later work repeatedly found this effect. Finkel examined changes in voting preference over the course of the 1980 campaign and showed that candidate preferences were remarkably stable and that when attitudes did change they invariably fit a pattern of partisan reinforcement or activation.[16] Gelman and King argued that information, one of the most important by-products of political campaigns, enables voters to choose according to their preferences.[17] As predicted by this "enlightenment" logic, Gelman and King found that voters assigned greater weight to "fundamental vari-

14. Bartels (1997a), p. 3; also see Petrocik (1996).
15. Lazarsfeld, Berelson, and Gaudet (1944).
16. Finkel (1993).
17. Gelman and King (1993).

ables" as the campaign progressed.[18] A similar pattern emerged in Holbrook's study of presidential campaigns, which found that candidates whose initial level of support lagged behind its predicted level (based on baseline variables such as partisanship, the incumbent's popularity, and the state of the economy) changed the most during the election cycle.[19] The campaign impact, then, was most notable for candidates who entered the race as "underachievers" with an initial level of support lagging their predicted level of support. The campaign effect primed the relevance of the fundamental variables of partisanship, incumbent popularity, and the state of the economy, producing a better fit between fundamental variables and voter choice.

Petrocik's analysis of the 1980 election yielded similar results: candidate preferences increasingly coincided with the issues and problems about which voters were concerned.[20] A related analysis of the 1988 election showed that George Bush's persistent emphasis on the peace and prosperity of the Reagan years caused voters' evaluations of the state of the country to become increasingly correlated with their vote intention—a shift that moved Bush from a deficit in May to a lead by the middle of the summer.[21] A study of the 1991 Pennsylvania Senate election showed a similar result.[22]

A final piece of evidence concerning partisan activation derives from a series of experiments administered by Ansolabehere and Iyengar.[23] In these tightly controlled studies, the experimental manipulation (typically exposure to a single campaign advertisement) significantly boosted the sponsoring candidate's level of support. More to the point, this effect was concentrated among voters who shared the partisanship of the sponsor. Thus the principal effect of campaign advertising was to strengthen party-line voting.[24]

Not all the individual-level survey evidence supports the hypothesis of partisan reinforcement. Examining all NES surveys since 1980, Bartels compiled evidence that amounted to "a resounding disconfirmation of the

---

18. Gelman and King used party affiliation and race as their indicators of the "fundamental variables."
19. Holbrook (1996).
20. Petrocik (1996).
21. Petrocik and Steeper (1989).
22. Blunt, Petrocik, and Steeper (1998).
23. Ansolabehere and Iyengar (1995).
24. Ansolabehere and Iyengar (1995), ch. 4.

partisan activation hypothesis, at least as it applies to the autumn campaign in recent presidential election years."[25] Using the date on which respondents were interviewed as a proxy for exposure to the campaign (respondents interviewed in early September were treated as less exposed than those surveyed in late October), Bartels found that neither the impact of party identification on vote choice nor the level of party identification itself was strengthened among respondents interviewed nearer election day.[26]

Basic Rule Voting as a Campaign Effect

This analysis focuses on how campaigns activate two fundamental political predispositions: partisanship and assessments of the job performance of the incumbent president. In any given election, we expect voters' choices to follow directly from their party affiliation; Democrats will vote Democratic, and Republicans will vote Republican. When the partisan cue is absent—for example, the voter is nonpartisan—voters turn to their evaluations of presidential performance: those who believe the president has done well vote for him (or the party's nominee), while those who rate the incumbent president's performance negatively vote for the challenger. Further, we expect these retrospective performance judgments to underlie the vote choices of defecting partisans.

Together, partisanship and the performance of the incumbent combine to produce the following basic rule for voters: vote party affiliation and defect according to the logic of incumbent approval, which is to say that you should vote for the other party's candidate only if you disapprove of the job performance of your party's incumbent or approve of the job performance of the other party's incumbent. Independents should vote according to their evaluation of the incumbent's job performance.

Using both experimental and survey-based indicators of exposure to the campaign, this analysis shows that campaigns boost the number of voters who choose according to the party/incumbent approval calculus of the basic rule.[27] It shows that the structuring effects of presidential cam-

25. Bartels (1997a), pp. 16–17.

26. This finding may reflect the confounding effect mentioned above: that is, the September to November period is not the relevant time frame for assessing contemporary campaigns.

27. Our basic voting rule has some affinities to the well-known "rule" articulated by Kelley and Mirer (1974) in that it expects the voter to consult partisanship and a compara-

paigns on vote choice are especially pronounced among young voters and weak partisans who lack the necessary commitments to engage in rule-based voting without the activation provided by campaigns. In concluding, we note that the controversy over structural versus campaign-oriented accounts of elections is artificial: party affiliation and assessments of presidential performance affect voter behavior because of the campaign.

A Research Design to Test Campaign Effects

Using experimental and national survey data from the 1992 and 1996 presidential campaigns (and survey data for some earlier races), we show that the basic voting rule provides a close approximation to observed voter behavior. More important, the data demonstrate that exposure to the campaign significantly increases the number of voters who choose consistent with the basic rule. The structural components of electoral choice are activated by exposure to the presidential campaign. Partisanship and voters' evaluations of presidential performance together account for the great majority of votes cast in recent presidential elections. Given the impact of incumbent approval on vote choice and the fact that performance is such a perennial campaign message, the campaign activation hypothesis leads us to expect a significant interaction between exposure to the campaign and evaluations of the incumbent president's job performance. Surprisingly, we know of no previous study that has examined this interaction directly, although Bartels's recent analysis of the effects of presidential campaigns on the weight that voters assign to their beliefs about the state of the economy provides a close approximation.[28]

---

tive candidate evaluation in deciding how to vote. However, the differences between the two are quite substantial. In Kelley and Mirer's rule the proximate and major determinant of the vote choice is a candidate evaluation based on diffuse likes and dislikes. Party identification is only consulted as a tie-breaker for partisans whose comparative candidate assessment is neutral. The basic voting rule articulated here is based on the demonstrated priority of party identification as a determinant of the vote. The candidate approval measure is used only to "explain" the decision of independents and defectors. Further, the candidate component of the Kelley-Mirer rule is a comparative assessment of feelings toward the candidates. The basic voting rule used here ignores the challenger. The candidate component of our basic voting rule is a retrospective assessment of only one candidate—the incumbent.

28. Bartels (1997a). This also was one of the results reported by Markus (1988). Bartels's examination of NES surveys since 1980 found that exposure to the presidential campaign more than doubled the impact of beliefs about the state of the economy on vote choice (see

Experiments and Surveys

The complementary advantages and disadvantages of experimentation and surveys provide compelling evidence for the validity of our results. Surveys can easily generalize to populations, but they are in a weak position to assess exposure to the campaign. Experiments, in contrast, can calibrate exposure precisely, but the generalizability of their results may be indeterminate. This analysis first tests the activation hypothesis experimentally, manipulating voters' level of exposure to the 1992 and 1996 campaigns, and then corroborates those results with survey data comparing the vote choices of respondents who were interviewed during the early and late stages of the campaign.

Experiments have liabilities. In many cases the subjects are "captive" (college students) who are not representative. More important for this study is that experiments usually occur in sterile laboratory-like environments. No experiment can reproduce the cacophony and confusion of election campaigns, particularly as they are experienced by people who lead busy lives in which political stimuli are only a small fraction of their daily experiences. But we took steps to enhance both the generalizability and realism of the campaign experiments.

The Campaign Experiments

The experiments contrast voters living in the Greater Los Angeles area who watched no television advertisement or news report about the presidential campaign with those who watched one or two campaign messages. Random assignment assured that participants were equivalent in all respects except "exposure" to the campaigns. Any observed difference between the experimental and control groups thus can be attributed to exposure.

The generalizability of our results was boosted by using a subject pool that was reasonably representative of the local (Southern California) voting-age population. Unlike the usual social science experiment, our participants were people from many walks of life and included adults of all ages, employed and unemployed, whites, African Americans, and Hispan-

Bartels 1997a, pp. 11–12). Over the course of the campaign, voters who believed the economy had improved (who, presumably, also approved of the president's performance), became even more likely to vote for the incumbent.

Table 6-1. *Profile of Experimental Participants, 1992 and 1996*
Percent unless otherwise noted

Characteristic	1992	1996
Median age (years)	33	37
Party identification		
Democrat	45	39
Republican	24	33
Independent	31	26
Race or ethnicity		
White	62	75
African American	20	8
Hispanic	9	8
Asian	8	5
Male	48	51

ics, men and women, city dwellers and suburbanites, and so forth (table 6-1 provides details on the socioeconomic and political composition of the participants). Participants were recruited by the use of flyers, announcements in newsletters, and personal contact in shopping malls offering payment of $15 for participation in "media research."

The realism of the design was strengthened by administering the experiments during actual campaigns. Our experiments all took place between August and early November, the period of the general election campaign. The messages included in our experiments were, in the great majority of conditions, actual campaign advertisements.[29] In addition to advertisements, some participants viewed "ad watch" reports in which a particular presidential candidate was scrutinized.

The experiments also attempted to heighten the mundane realism of the real-world experience of exposure to campaign advertising. The aura of the experimental laboratory was diminished by designing the viewing environment to resemble, as closely as possible, the normal conditions in which a person views television. Comfortable couches and chairs were arranged in front of a television set, with houseplants and wall hangings placed around the room. Respondents were offered coffee, cookies, and soft drinks to enjoy during the viewing sessions. In most cases, family

29. In 1992 one of the advertising conditions featured a Bill Clinton ad dealing with issues of women's rights. We created this ad using footage from the Hill-Thomas hearings and from other Clinton ads.

members or friends took part in the experiment at the same time, so that respondents did not find themselves sitting next to a stranger while viewing the videotape.[30]

The sites selected for each experiment were virtually identical in layout and decor. Each site consisted of a two-room office suite located in or near a retail shopping area. One of the rooms was used for viewing the tapes, and the other was used for filling out questionnaires. The 1992 experiments were conducted at two sites. The first was located near Westwood, a predominantly liberal and Democratic neighborhood located just south of the University of California, Los Angeles, campus. The other was located in Costa Mesa, a small city in more conservative Orange County. In 1996 the design included three sites. One was in a popular shopping mall in Westwood. The second was in a small shopping area in Moorpark, a northern suburb of Los Angeles. The third site was located in Manhattan Beach, a coastal city south of Los Angeles. This variety of locations helped to diversify the subject pool.

The Design of the Experiments

We used two different experimental designs. The first (administered during the 1992 campaign) embedded the campaign message (either an advertisement or an ad watch report) into a fifteen-minute recording of a recent local newscast. Because candidates advertise heavily during local news programs, the appearance of the experimental campaign advertisement in the local newscast was inconspicuous. All other news stories and product advertisements were screened so that they were not relevant to the campaign, and these same filler stories and ads were used in combination with each political advertisement. Within this "newscast" design, participants were exposed to either one or two campaign advertisements from the presidential candidates. However, in no case did participants watch more than one spot from a particular candidate.

The majority (five) of the advertising conditions in the 1992 experiments featured messages dealing with the state of the economy. Bill Clinton attacked George Bush's record on the economy, promoted his own economic plan, and described the "Arkansas miracle." For his part, Bush described his economic goals for a second term (lower taxes, more open

---

30. Although participants were free to converse with each other during the viewing sessions, they completed their responses to the questionnaires individually, often in separate rooms.

export markets, a lower deficit) and attacked Clinton as a "tax and spend liberal." A sixth condition emphasized Clinton's support for women's rights (featuring the Anita Hill–Clarence Thomas hearings and Clinton's pro-choice stance). Finally, we used a pair of advertisements concerning the "character" issue—the Clinton advertisement "Journey" and a Bush spot emphasizing the importance of trust and integrity.

Three of the conditions during the 1992 study featured ad watch reports. In the first, CNN (Cable News Network) reporter Brooks Jackson critiqued the "Arkansas miracle" advertisement describing Clinton's accomplishments while governor. A second report focused on the Clinton advertisement ("In His Own Words") attacking Bush's performance on the economy. Finally, we used a third report (also by Jackson) dealing with the accuracy of a Bush advertisement attacking Clinton for raising taxes while governor of Arkansas.

The control condition in 1992 consisted of participants who watched a newscast with no campaign advertisements as well as participants who watched a newscast that included one or more ads from one of the U.S. Senate campaigns in California. As we will show, the initial results indicated that these two groups were similar in the degree to which participants supported candidates according to the basic rule. They thus were combined, and the design was reduced to conditions that featured a message from the presidential campaign and conditions that did not.[31]

In 1996 we used a different design in which participants simply watched a videotaped collection of nine television advertisements, one of which was an advertisement from the 1996 presidential campaign.[32] The experimental treatments corresponded to the actual advertisements being aired in Southern California by Clinton and Bob Dole.[33] The particular advertisements used addressed illegal immigration, drug abuse, the budget defi-

31. The California senatorial campaigns of 1992 featured two high-profile races: Barbara Boxer (Democrat) versus Bruce Herschensohn (Republican) in one and Dianne Feinstein (Democrat) versus John Seymour (Republican) in the other. The experimental advertisements featured in the Senate studies covered a variety of subjects including women's rights (1992 was the "year of the woman"), crime and urban unrest, the depressed state of the California economy, and others. For a more detailed description of the studies and stimulus materials used in the 1992 Senate studies, see Ansolabehere and Iyengar (1995).

32. The ads appearing in the tape (in order) were sponsored by the following products or companies: Kentucky Fried Chicken, United Airlines, Advil, Nicorette, Yuban, Advantage Flea Control, AT&T, Jack-in-the-Box, and Ford.

33. In general, we synchronized our participants' exposure to the 1996 ads with the candidates' ad buys.

cit, crime, federal spending on social welfare programs, the state of the economy, taxes, and "character."

In two other experimental conditions, participants watched a collection of three news stories, one of which was an ad watch dealing with either a Clinton or a Dole advertisement.[34] The first covered the Dole ad on drug abuse among juveniles, and the second focused on Clinton's advertisement "Wrong in the Past," which attacked Senator Dole's previous opposition to social security and other benefit programs.

Finally, the "no message" control group in 1996 consisted of participants who watched no political advertisement or news report at all and those participants who watched an advertisement either supporting or opposing Proposition 209—the California Civil Rights Initiative.[35] The proportion of participants in these two sets of conditions who voted "structurally" was virtually identical and significantly different from the corresponding proportion in the "presidential campaign" conditions. As in the case of 1992, the design was reduced to two levels—participants who received a message from the presidential campaign and those who did not.[36]

The Survey Data

Survey data were drawn from the 1980, 1988, 1992, and 1996 presidential elections. The 1980 and 1988 data were used to corroborate patterns observed in 1992 and 1996. We began with the latter two elections because the experimental data were collected in 1992 and 1996.

In addition to the surveys carried out by the NES for 1992 and 1996, we included pre-campaign national surveys (administered in May 1992 and February 1996) carried out by organizations associated with the Bush and Dole campaigns, respectively.[37] The questions concerning vote inten-

34. The two noncampaign stories on the tape concerned the illness of the pope and the efforts of a small college in Kentucky to provide students with employment opportunities.

35. Proposition 209, which was passed by the electorate, required state agencies to terminate preferential consideration based on race or gender.

36. The "voting" that is described in the experiments is actually a vote intention and not a reported vote. In our estimation the intention is functionally equivalent to a reported and observed vote since what the design tests is whether campaign exposure increases behavior or, in the case of the experiments, "intended behavior" that is consistent with the basic rule of candidate evaluation and support.

37. The non-NES data are standard telephone surveys that were stratified by region. In addition to sample design weights, the data sets are weighted to ensure proper proportions of key demographic groups, with special attention to the distribution of age, gender, and race.

tion, presidential approval, party identification, and age were essentially identical in these studies. The survey data do not fully replicate the exposure manipulation in the experiments. We approximated the manipulation by stratifying respondents according to when they were interviewed, assuming that respondents interviewed nearer the election experienced more campaign activity than those interviewed early in the election season. For the 1992 campaign, we compared the rates of party voting and basic rule voting in May (before the campaign) with the corresponding rates for two periods during the fall campaign—September and October. The analysis of the 1996 campaign relied on a similar comparison: party and basic rule voting before the campaign (February) versus after the onset of the campaign.

Following the presentation of the parallel survey results for 1992 and 1996, we broadened the investigation to encompass the 1980 and 1988 campaigns (1984 was excluded because we had no national surveys covering a comparable time frame). All of the 1980 data were drawn from the more elaborate NES study of that year; separate surveys were administered in January, June, July, and the standard September-October sampling frame. Finally, the data for 1988 were drawn from surveys carried out for the Bush campaign (administered in May, July, and early September), from the 1988 NES September-October survey, and from a Republican-sponsored survey conducted during the week immediately after the election.

Indicators

Our indicator of candidate preference was the respondent's vote intention. In the experiments we asked participants (following the playing of the videotape), "If the election were held today, how would you vote?" A similar question in the surveys assessed candidate preference at the time of the interview. Responses to this question were coded as a dichotomy with intended votes for the Democrat set equal to +1 and votes for the Republican set to 0. For the analysis of the 1992 and 1996 elections, we tested the activation hypothesis both with and without Ross Perot voters. Most of the analysis reported below excludes Perot voters. Perot supporters were included at one point to demonstrate that the net effect of excluding them is to depress the magnitude of the differences observed as a function of campaign exposure.

Professed party identification and a measure of incumbent job approval are the structural determinants of the vote.[38] Of course, incumbent approval is contaminated by partisanship, making it difficult to disentangle party voting from approval voting. However, our operationalization of the basic voting rule forces party identification and approval of the incumbent to be mutually exclusive: job approval is relevant only for independents and partisan defectors. By definition, independents cannot assess the incumbent through a partisan lens. Similarly, a Democrat who disapproved of Clinton's job performance in 1996 or a Republican who disapproved of Bush's job performance in 1992 cannot be rationalizing partisanship because their assessment of the president is contrary to the partisan connection. The votes of partisan defectors, accordingly, can be attributed purely to the approval component of the basic voting rule.

In sum, we used a composite of partisanship and approval of the incumbent's performance to classify voters who responded to structural factors.[39] The responsiveness of the voter to structural influences was measured first in terms of simple party voting and second in terms of both partisanship and incumbent approval. Table 6-2 summarizes the measures. The party voting rule focuses exclusively on partisans and stipulates that they vote accordingly: Republicans for Bush in 1992 and Dole in 1996

38. Experimental participants were asked to indicate their party affiliation: "Generally speaking, do you think of yourself as a Republican, a Democrat, an independent, or what?" Later, they were asked the incumbent approval question: "How would you rate ___'s overall performance as president?" Responses were recorded on a scale ranging from 1 (very good) to 7 (very poor). We trichotomized responses into positive (1 through 3), negative (5 through 7), and neutral (all other) categories. In 1992 the party identification and incumbent approval questions were both asked before exposure to the campaign message. Therefore, our estimates of campaign activation are not contaminated by any message-induced changes in partisanship or popularity. Any experimental effects can only be due to participants adjusting their vote preferences to match these structural cues. In 1996 the incumbent approval question was moved to the post-test. To test for any traces of movement in approval, we compared the mean approval rating for participants in the presidential and nonpresidential campaigns. There was no difference in the level of approval. Thus, in both experimental tests, we can be confident that the structural factors are in fact related to vote choice. Survey respondents were asked the standard party identification and presidential approval questions. Leaners are defined as partisans of the party toward which they lean. Only those who insist that they feel close to neither party are classified as independents. See Petrocik (1989); Keith and others (1992).

39. Approval voting can be based on the actual incumbent or, if neither candidate is the incumbent, on the voter's evaluation of the performance of the retiring incumbent. In these situations, the candidate of the same party as the incumbent is rewarded or burdened by the voter's judgment (assessments of Reagan mattered for Bush and Dukakis in 1988; satisfaction with Clinton will matter in 2000).

Table 6-2. *Party and Basic Rule Voting*

Rule	Prediction
The party rule	Party identification is consistent with vote choice
The basic rule	Party identification is consistent with vote choice, or defection is consistent with incumbent job assessment, or independents' vote choice is consistent with incumbent job assessment

and Democrats for Clinton.[40] Defectors are treated as violating the party rule. The party rule makes no prediction, obviously, for independents.

Basic rule voting encompasses party voting for partisans and adds retrospective approval of the incumbent for independents and party defectors. Defectors and independents conform to structural influences if their vote choice corresponds to their assessment of the performance of the incumbent president. An independent or Republican who voted for Clinton in 1992, for example, is regarded as a basic rule voter if he or she disapproved of Bush's performance as president.

Results

The key test of the campaign activation hypothesis is the amount of change that occurs in the rate of party and basic rule voting in 1992 and 1996 as a result of exposure to the presidential campaign. In the experiments, the proportion of party and basic rule voters should be greater among individuals exposed to a campaign advertisement or ad watch. In the surveys, where time of interview is a proxy for campaign exposure, the proportion of party and basic rule voters will increase over time.

We begin by examining the separate contributions of each structural factor—party identification and incumbent approval—to the vote choices of participants in the experiments. Table 6-3 presents, by year, the percentage of participants within each of the three levels of the experimental design (corresponding to the presidential, nonpresidential, and no-message conditions) whose vote intentions were classified accurately on the basis of their party identity and evaluations of the incumbent's job performance.

40. Those intending to vote for Ross Perot are deleted from the base. This was done to maximize comparability with the experimental data. This decision tends to suppress the effect of the campaign. Including Perot voters in the analysis increases the effect of the campaign, as figure 6-2 and table 6-4 make clear.

Table 6-3. *Elements of Structural Voting in the 1992 and 1996 Campaign Experiments*
Percent

Year and condition	Voting consistent with	
	Party identification	Approval of incumbent
1992		
Presidential ads	73	72
No ads	70	69
Senate ads	69	64
Effect of manipulation (F)	n.s.	< 0.01
1996		
Presidential ads	79	88
No ads	73	88
Senate ads	74	89
Effect of manipulation (F)	< 0.11	n.s.

n.s. Not significant.

In both years, participants who were exposed to the campaign ads registered the highest level of party-based voting, although the differences approached significance ($p < 0.11$) only in 1996. Approval-based voting also peaked in the presidential campaign conditions. Here, the differences were significant in 1992 ($p < 0.01$) and not in 1996.

From our perspective, the most important feature of table 6-3 is the behavior of the participants exposed to a nonpresidential campaign message; in all four comparisons, their presidential voting choices were either equally or less predictable than the choices made by the participants who saw no campaign message. This pattern suggests that exposure to a message from some other campaign is functionally equivalent to no message at all, at least in terms of the logic of campaign activation. We thus collapsed the no-message and nonpresidential message conditions in both years; the analyses that follow rely on this reduced form of the manipulation.

The full-fledged test of the campaign activation hypothesis presumes that candidate preference is a joint function of party affiliation and incumbent approval (the basic rule). Partisans vote for their party, and nonpartisans vote according to how they evaluate the incumbent's performance, as do defecting partisans. Figure 6-1 summarizes the experimental and survey evidence for 1992 and 1996.

The experiments produced significant activation of party voting in 1996 ($p < 0.05$) and measurable but statistically weaker increases in 1992. In

Figure 6-1. *Campaign Effects on Voting: Experimental and Survey Results, 1992 and 1996*

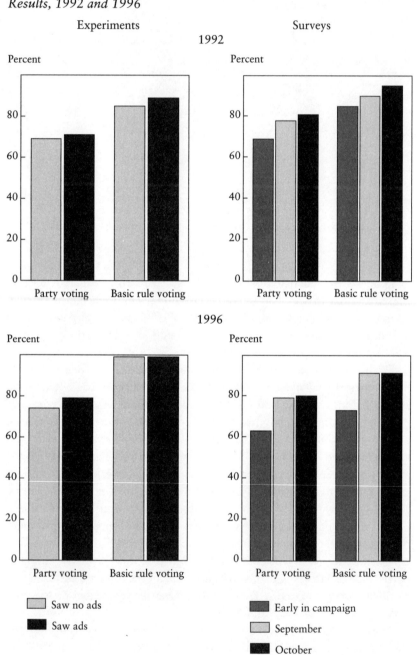

the case of basic rule voting, the campaign activation effect was significant in 1992 ($p < 0.05$), but the utter predictability of participants' vote choices in 1996 from the basic rule precluded further activation—the share voting consistent with the basic rule remained fixed at 98 percent. Thus even among participants who were shielded from the presidential campaign, 1996 vote choice was fully accounted for by party and incumbent approval. Under these circumstances, exposure to the campaign had no impact in the experiments.

The September-October NES survey data are strikingly comparable to the level of basic rule voting that occurred after the subjects were exposed to the experimental manipulation and parallel the experiments quite closely at significant points. First, there is substantial similarity (perhaps fortuitous) in the actual proportions of basic rule voters in the experiments and the surveys. In May 1992 approximately 70 percent of the two-party vote division for president was purely partisan (the exact result obtained in the experiment). When we count nonpartisans and defectors who voted according to their evaluations of Bush's performance, the percentage of "correct" votes increased to 86 percent. The pattern was similar in 1996. In February of that year, 64 percent of the sample intended to vote consistent with their partisanship and 74 percent with the basic rule, despite the fact that it was so early in the election year that respondents were unsure about the likely Republican nominee.

Second, the effect of the campaigns is apparent, despite the high level of pre-campaign candidate preference in both years. Even though most of the increase in party and basic rule voting occurred between the pre-campaign observation and September, party voting was activated further during September and October 1992 ($p < 0.10$). In the case of 1996, however, neither party nor basic rule voting increased after September. Thus, according to both the experimental and survey data, post-September campaign activation occurred only in 1992.

Third, the experimental and survey data also converge on the result that virtually all the activation in structure-based voting occurred in partisan voting. The retrospective, incumbent-approval component of the basic rule was constant from May to November in 1992 and from February to November in 1996. In the 1992 experiments, most of the exposure-induced increase in basic rule voting was an increase in party voting. For the 1992 surveys, all of the increase in basic rule voting occurred because of heightened consistency between party identification and vote intention. There was a net decrease in basic rule voting between May and October

Table 6-4. *Components of Basic Rule Voting in 1992 and 1996 Surveys*
Percent

Date	Party	Approval	Total[a]
1992			
May	70	16	86
September	78	14	92
October	81	14	95
1996			
February	64	11	75
September	78	9	87
October	78	11	89

a. Equals the proportion of the sample casting a vote consistent with the component or rule.

(see table 6-4). In 1996 campaign-induced increases in party voting similarly overwhelmed approval voting. The performance evaluations contributed not at all to the activation effect in the 1996 experiments; they also added nothing to the predictability of the overall vote between the February and November surveys.

Finally, the survey data suggest that presidential campaigning seems to decide the election *before* September (supporting one of the explanations for why so little campaign effect is observed in September and October). Most of the vote in 1992 and 1996 was decided well before the onset of the fall campaign. The approval component, in particular, was invariant after September, although the party component also changed very little. The events that occurred during the first three quarters of the campaign year brought into line virtually all of the individuals who were to vote consistent with the basic voting rule. The fall campaign only reinforced the earlier result.

The Perot Vote

A distinctive characteristic of the 1992 and 1996 campaigns was the candidacy of Ross Perot. The presence of a strong third-party candidate may, at first glance, be expected to undermine the role of party voting. But in fact, the inclusion of Perot only serves to highlight the campaign's strong activation of partisan predispositions. Figure 6-2 documents the extent of partisan mobilization in the 1992 survey data with Perot voters included. Figure 6-2 differs from figure 6-1 by (1) counting an intention to vote for

Figure 6-2. *Basic Rule Voting in 1992, Counting Perot Voters*

Percent

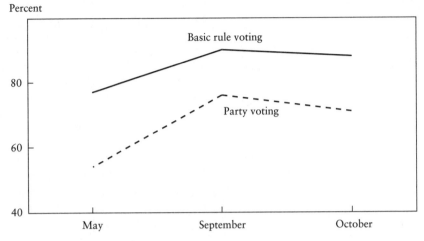

Perot as a violation of the party rule and (2) counting a vote for Ross Perot as consistent with the basic voting rule for defecting Republican identifiers and independents who disapproved of Bush's performance.

With Perot's vote counted, only about 54 percent of the sample had a voting intention that was consistent with their party identification in May. The remaining 46 percent represented independents (about 10 percent) and defectors, with most of the defectors expressing a preference for the insurgent Perot rather than the major-party alternative to their party's candidate. The retrospective dimension of the basic voting rule explained about half of the defection rate. Thus about 23 percent (100 – 77, see the last column of table 6-5) of the expressed vote intention in May 1992 was inconsistent with either the partisan or retrospective dimension of the basic voting rule. Between May and the start of the fall campaign in September, this figure fell to 10 percent (100 – 90). All of this change occurred because of an increase in the party voting component of the basic voting rule: party voting increased about 22 percent (from 54 to 76 percent). The impact of incumbent approval on the vote declined between May and September. While 23 percent of the respondents were voting for a candidate on exclusively retrospective grounds in May, by September only 14 percent were casting purely retrospective votes. Table 6-5 shows quite clearly that the campaign mobilized partisans. The incumbent approval

Table 6-5. *Components of Basic Rule Voting in 1992 with Ross Perot Supporters Included*
Percent

Date	Party	Approval	Total[a]
May	54	23	77
September	76	14	90
October	67	19	86

a. Equals the proportion of the sample casting a vote consistent with the component or rule.

dimension of the basic voting rule was in place well before the presidential campaign reached its maximum intensity. Retrospective voters made their decisions early; but the campaign, by activating partisanship, actually pulled a substantial 40 percent of May approval voters back to a party vote.

In summary, the experimental and survey data both reveal significant campaign activation in 1992 and 1996. Party and approval-based voting both increased as a result of exposure to the campaign. The activation effect was especially pronounced in the case of party voting, with or without counting Perot supporters. The presence of a third candidate provided more latitude for the campaign to activate partisanship, although party voting declined as the Perot campaign made inroads into Democratic and Republican ranks (figure 6-2).

Confirming the Pattern: 1980 and 1988

The experimental and survey data for the pair of Clinton elections match quite closely. But is this pair of elections atypical, and is the agreement between the surveys and the experiments fortuitous? To extend the generalizability of the results, we considered the 1980 and 1988 campaigns. Again, 1984 was excluded because we have no national survey covering a comparable time frame.

As shown in figure 6-3, the changes observed with the 1980 NES panel study and a series of surveys conducted during the 1988 presidential election year are virtually identical to those observed in the Clinton elections.

In January 1980, when many voters were undecided and neither party, but especially the Republican party, had a certain nominee, less than 50 percent of the public had a preference that was consistent with the party rule and only 60 percent expressed a preference that was consistent with

Figure 6-3. *Basic Rule Voting in 1980 and 1988*

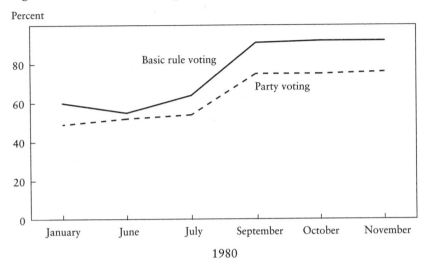

Percent

Basic rule voting

Party voting

January   June   July   September   October   November

1980

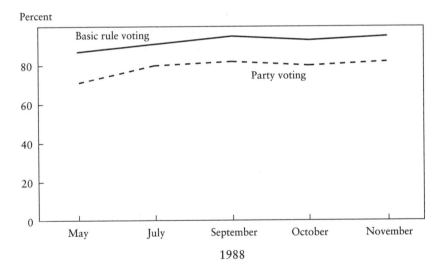

Percent

Basic rule voting

Party voting

May   July   September   October   November

1988

the two-part basic voting rule. By mid-summer, at which time Jimmy Carter and Ronald Reagan had secured their nomination, the number of party voters increased to about 55 percent, and voters choosing by the basic rule increased to 64 percent. Those figures increased to about 66 and 91 percent, respectively, by September, where they remained through October.

Table 6-6. *Components of Basic Rule Voting in 1980 and 1988*
Percent

Date	Party	Approval	Total[a]
1980			
January	49	11	60
June	52	3	55
July	55	11	64
September	76	15	91
October	76	17	93
Reported vote	77	16	93
1988			
May	71	11	82
July	80	11	91
Early September	82	13	95
NES (September/October)	80	13	93
Reported vote	82	11	95

a. Equals the proportion of the sample casting a vote consistent with the component or rule.

The pattern of results for 1988 was virtually identical. Michael Dukakis led Bush through the end of July. Just over 70 percent of the electorate had preferences that were consistent with the party rule, and 81 percent could be classified as basic rule voters. By mid-August, a combination of increased party and approval-based voting put Bush into a dead heat, where the contest remained through September (a result corroborated by the September NES interviews). By October, Bush had forged a six-point lead among voters who had decided whom they would support; party voting was just over 80 percent, and basic rule voting reached 93 percent. The vote intention remained at that margin through election day, when Bush defeated Dukakis with 53 percent of the vote, with a basic rule vote of 95 percent and a party vote of 83 percent.

The changes in the party and approval components of the basic voting rule in 1980 and 1988 were substantially similar in magnitude to those observed in 1992 and 1996 (table 6-6). That is, the activation effect of the campaign was larger for party voting than for approval-based voting. The total activation effect was especially strong in 1980, but three-quarters (forty-five points versus thirteen points) of the increase in basic rule voting between January and September-October were contributed by the mobilization of partisans. In 1988 the overall activation effects were much smaller—there was only a thirteen-point increase in basic rule voting (compared with 58 percent in 1980)—but, once again, partisan mobilization outweighed mobilization of retrospective voters by a ratio of better than five to one.

Two themes recur in these results. First, campaigns do activate structural variables, and this effect is unlikely to be observed during the fall because most of the change occurs before September. Sometimes the activation effect is very large (as it was in 1980); at other times it is negligible (as it was in 1996). The changes that do occur during the fall campaign may decide the election (as happened in 1980 and 1988), but the magnitude of the shift is sufficiently small to make its detection difficult.

Second, campaigns prime the partisan component of structural voting to a greater degree than evaluations of the incumbent's performance. If the performance evaluation captures the dynamic elements of the campaign on which the incumbent or challenger hopes to capitalize, it is clearly the smaller component of the vote and of whatever changes occur. It seems that the most retrospectively motivated voters make early and firm judgments about the performance of the incumbent, and the campaign produces very little further activation of approval judgments.

Who Is Influenced?

Our final set of analyses focused on the differential role of campaigns for voters with little, some, or extensive past experience with party and basic rule voting. We focused on age (in the experiments) and strength of partisanship (in the surveys).[41]

We anticipated that older voters—who have had repeated opportunities to vote and who have a more entrenched bond with their party—would find the campaign redundant; they "know" how to vote without prompting from the candidates. In psychological terms, they are chronic structure-bound voters. Conversely, we anticipated that relatively inexperienced voters, those with only one previous presidential campaign under their belt, would be the most in "need" of activation. Lacking the experience to fall back on structural factors as a matter of habit, these voters are brought into line by the campaign. In short, we expected a significant interaction between age and exposure to the experimental manipulation:

---

41. The different indicators were necessary because the experimental questionnaire did not include strength of party identification. Age was used as a proxy for strength of partisanship.

younger voters will register the greatest increase in structural voting as a result of exposure to the campaign.

The experimental results on exposure to the campaign, age, and party voting are arrayed in figure 6-4. In 1992 the effects of the campaign were much stronger among the young. Participants under the age of twenty-eight registered a twelve-point increase in party voting compared with an average increase of 3 percent for the two older groups. This divergence produced a significant interaction ($p < 0.05$) between exposure to the campaign and age. The results for basic rule voting were identical; exposure to the campaign had little impact on the votes of middle-age or older voters but produced a ten-point increase among the young. Once again, the age and exposure to the campaign condition proved significant ($p < 0.05$).

The pattern was less striking in 1996. Exposure to the campaign had the largest impact on party voting among the youngest group of participants. However, the age-related differential in the effects of exposure was insufficiently large to warrant a significant interaction effect. In the case of basic rule voting, all three age groups exhibited full conformity to the rule even among participants not exposed to the campaign, thus precluding any possible effects of exposure.

In the survey data, we can examine differences in party voting as a function of the strength of respondents' partisanship. Figure 6-5 plots the rate of party and basic rule voting for 1992 and 1996 by strength of identification (which was approximated in the experiments by age).[42] The survey data do not corroborate the experimental results fully, although the pattern is consistent. In particular, the main theoretical result of the experimental data is strongly confirmed: party and basic rule voting changed more over the course of the election season among weak partisans and independents than they did among strong identifiers. Strong partisans exhibited very high rates of party voting regardless of the stage of the campaign. In 1992, 89 percent of the strong partisans interviewed in May intended to cast a party vote; in 1996 this figure was 88 percent as early as February. While party voting among strong partisans increased seven to

42. Independents, in addition to leaners and weak identifiers, are grouped as weak partisans in figures 6-5 and 6-6 and in table 6-6. This was done to maintain maximum comparability between these presentations and earlier tables and graphs. The absolute values for party and basic rule voting are reduced by this decision, but the slopes for the weak partisans are unchanged. The inclusion of independents has *no* effect on the relationship between exposure to the campaign and basic rule voting.

Figure 6-4. *Voting by Age and Campaign Exposure, 1992 and 1996*

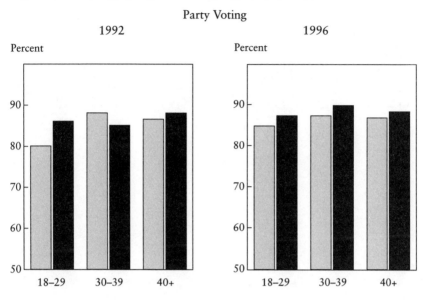

Party Voting

1992 1996

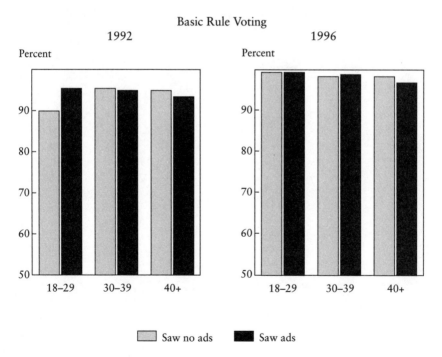

Basic Rule Voting

1992 1996

Saw no ads   Saw ads

Figure 6-5. *Voting by Strength of Partisanship, 1992 and 1996*

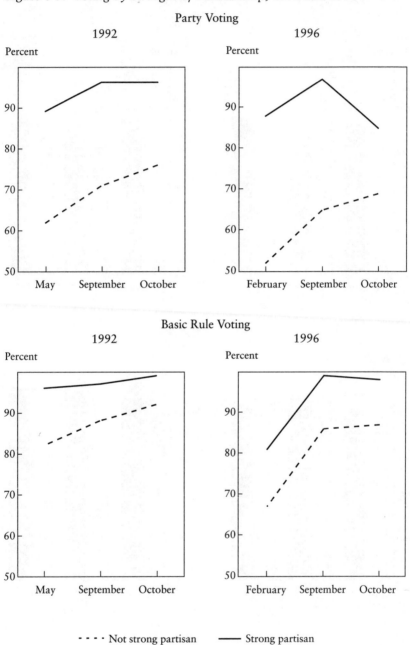

Party Voting

1992   1996

Percent   Percent

Basic Rule Voting

1992   1996

Percent   Percent

- - - - Not strong partisan   ——— Strong partisan

Table 6-7. *Rate of Change from Early Measurements to the Fall in Party Voting and Basic Rule Voting, 1992 and 1996*

Partisanship	Party voting	Basic rule voting
1992		
Strong	+7	+3
Weak	+12	+9
1996		
Strong	+8	+8
Weak	+16	+21

eight percentage points by September and October of the election year, the change was almost twice as large among weak partisans. The pattern was essentially identical for basic rule voting. In 1992 basic rule voting increased nine points among weak partisans ($p < 0.05$) compared with an insignificant three-point change among strong partisans. In 1996 basic rule voting increased twenty-one points among weak partisans and independents, but only eight points among strong partisans. Table 6-7 summarizes these changes.

The only real discrepancy between the experimental results and the survey data concerns the 1996 election. The experiments produced significant change in party voting overall in 1996, but the effect was not concentrated among the young. The survey data also revealed substantial changes over time in party voting, and the effects were enhanced among weak partisans. We can only speculate about the origins of this difference. The most likely reason is the different times at which the data were collected. The experiments were administered during August, September, and October, long after most Americans had reached their equilibrium presidential choice (as the survey data show). The effects of the campaign revealed in the survey data are based on a comparison of the electorate's vote intentions in February and September-October. In February, many Americans, but especially those who were not strongly partisan, were undecided or prepared to consider a vote that was inconsistent with the party rule. Between February and the fall of 1996 most of this inconsistency and indecision was resolved in favor of rule-based voting. The experiments, however, were conducted after this settling had rallied young and old participants alike firmly behind their party's nominee.

Partisan Differences in Activation in 1980 and 1988

The 1980 and 1988 elections allow us to replicate the pattern observed in 1992 and 1996. In general, as figure 6-6 shows, the pattern in these elections duplicates what was observed in 1992 and 1996. There is one striking difference: changes in party voting over the course of the 1980 campaign were as large among strong partisans as they were among weak partisans. The difference could reflect campaigning differences—the data do not span identical time periods, but the most likely cause is the large pro-Reagan surge that accompanied the certainty of his nomination. Republican defection to Carter was very high early in 1980, giving the president a substantial lead over his Republican challengers. In mid-1980 these Republican defectors surged into their partisan column, and the data reflect this shift.

This difference between the surveys notwithstanding, the similarity of the activation is striking. Weak partisans and independents registered substantially larger gains in party and basic rule voting. Overall, the survey results hold steady across elections. In each instance, exposure to the campaign proved most influential for weak partisans; as the campaign progresses, these voters "catch up" with their more committed counterparts. The experimental results suggest a similar pattern with age (at least in 1992): exposure to campaign advertising facilitates party or basic rule voting among the young.

Conclusions

Taken together, the experimental and survey evidence indicate that campaigns bring voters' candidate preferences into alignment with their partisanship and evaluations of the incumbent's performance. The most frequent manifestation of campaign activation is the shepherding of wayward or undecided partisans back into the fold. Weak partisans and others for whom electoral choice is a relatively novel undertaking are especially "protected." In this respect, our results mirror the considerable body of research that points to the reinforcing (rather than converting) effects of campaigns and the special responsiveness (to campaign messages) of those who are less involved; demonstrating again that campaigns are most "needed by," and have the largest effect on, political "have-nots."

Although campaigns activate both elements of the basic rule—partisanship and evaluations of the incumbent's performance—partisanship shows greater elasticity. We suspect that the prominence of the party com-

Figure 6-6. *Voting by Strength of Partisanship, 1980 and 1988*

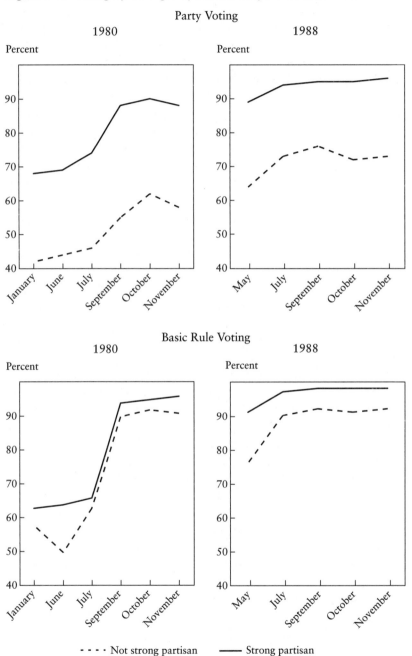

Party Voting

1980   1988

Basic Rule Voting

1980   1988

- - - - Not strong partisan ——— Strong partisan

ponent stems from the preference of candidates and strategists for waging campaigns aimed at their partisan base. Holding one's partisan base is the sine qua non of successful campaigning, and there is no better way to do this than to emphasize issues that represent the core programmatic commitments of the party.[43] For Democrats, this requires an emphasis on social welfare issues (child care, education, social security), racial equality, the fair treatment of labor unions, and so on; for Republicans it requires an emphasis on excessive taxation, the need for smaller government and more individual initiative, military preparedness, and increased crime control. In this sense, the equilibrium outcome of campaigning is for Democrats and Republicans to emphasize "owned" issues.[44] That is, campaign rhetoric is designed to remind voters of their policy stereotypes of the Republicans and Democrats.

The experimental studies provide us with considerable confidence that the logic of "ownership" mediates the activation of party affiliation. In 1996 we asked participants to rate the credibility of the "target" campaign ad; their responses showed that Democratic voters rated ads dealing with Democrat-owned issues (unemployment, civil rights, social welfare benefits) as most credible, while Republicans were especially impressed by ads dealing with crime, illegal immigration, and a balanced budget.[45] In sum, activation of partisanship during campaigns follows inevitably from the incentives facing voters and candidates.

The evidence concerning campaign-induced partisan activation has clear normative implications. In recent years, there has been no end of hand wringing and condemnation of modern campaigns for their use of deceptive and nonsubstantive messages that manipulate voters by distracting them from the "real" issues of the day. Perhaps this conventional wisdom has underestimated the political savvy of the electorate; when voters are swayed, the effect is invariably toward the "correct" (for example, partisan or retrospective) direction. Most scholars agree that party voting is sensible and allows voters to overcome their low levels of information about specific policies and candidate positions. Even if some voters are misled, the cumulative effect of campaigns is to enable the large majority of voters to cast ballots that reflect their political predispositions rather than the momentary appeal of a political advertisement. More than 90 percent of those intending to vote behave consistently with their most

---

43. See Petrocik (1996); Ansolabehere and Iyengar (1995).
44. See Simon (1998).
45. Iyengar and Valentino (forthcoming).

reliable long-term predisposition—party identification—and with a relevant short-term cue that is based on the logic of political accountability.[46] With so many voters casting "substantive" votes, the evidence suggests that campaigns are at least as likely to enlighten as to manipulate. The issue that is neither resolved nor even addressed by this finding is whether campaigns that activate long-term predispositions and depress the influence of short-term considerations are always desirable.

Finally, our evidence provides an explanation for the typical null result obtained by campaign researchers who rely on NES surveys. Virtually all of the shifting we observed in party and basic rule voting occurred before September. The primary campaign and the events that follow the emergence of a nominee seem sufficient to activate party and retrospective voting among the great majority of the electorate.[47] The size of this majority, of course, depends on circumstance. In 1996 the "campaign" actually may have begun in 1994 with the election of the Republican-controlled U.S. House of Representatives. The ensuing implementation of the Contract with America, repeated and prolonged policy impasses between Congress and President Clinton, the resulting shutdowns of the federal government, and the never-ending charges and countercharges over who did what to whom mobilized partisans very early in the run-up to the presidential contest. With repeated and continuous exposure to shrill partisan conflict, it is no surprise that by September, virtually everyone (98 percent in the experiments) was sufficiently informed about the candidates to engage in rule-based voting. In 1992, however, there were more "unknowns" surrounding the candidacy of Bill Clinton and the themes that defined the Bush and Clinton campaigns did not fall into place until after the nominating conventions. Since the onset of the campaign was relatively recent, both the experiments and fall surveys in 1992 revealed traces of post-September activation.

The bottom line, of course, is that the added value generated by any particular fall campaign is inversely related to the time voters have had before the fall to consider the candidates and the issues. The lesson for survey researchers in pursuit of campaign effects is that efforts to monitor public opinion must encompass more than the final stages of the campaign.

---

46. See Zaller (1998) for an argument that voters are responsible and not as swayed by political trivia as is generally believed.

47. The methodological implications of "long" campaigns are discussed in Bartels (1997b).

References

Abramowitz, Alan I. 1988. "An Improved Model for Predicting Presidential Elections." *Political Science and Politics* 2 (4): 843–46.

———. 1996. "Bill and Al's Excellent Adventure: Forecasting the 1996 Election." *American Politics Quarterly* 24 (4): 434–42.

Alvarez, R. Michael, and Jonathan Nagler. 1995. "Economics, Issues, and the Perot Candidacy: Voter Choice in the 1992 Presidential Election." *American Journal of Political Science* 39 (3): 714–44.

Ansolabehere, Stephen, and Shanto Iyengar. 1995. *Going Negative: How Political Advertisements Shrink and Polarize the Electorate.* Free Press.

Ansolabehere, Stephen, Shanto Iyengar, Adam Simon, and Nicholas Valentino. 1994. "Does Attack Advertising Demobilize the Electorate?" *American Political Science Review* 88 (4): 829–38.

Bartels, Larry M. 1992. "Electioneering in the United States." In David Butler and Austin Ranney, eds., *Electioneering: A Comparative Study of Continuity and Change.* Oxford University Press.

———. 1993. "Messages Received: The Political Impact of Media Exposure." *American Political Science Review* 87 (2): 267–85.

———. 1997a. "How Campaigns Matter." Paper presented at the annual meeting of the American Political Science Association, Washington, D.C., August.

———. 1997b. "Three Virtues of Panel Data for the Analysis of Campaign Effects." Paper prepared for the conference on campaign effects, University of British Columbia, Vancouver, B.C.

Blunt, Christopher C., John R. Petrocik, and Frederick T. Steeper. 1998. "Priming and Issue Agenda in American Campaigns: Wofford vs. Thornburgh in the 1991 Pennsylvania Senate Race." Paper presented at the annual meeting of the Midwest Political Science Association, Chicago, April.

Bradshaw, Joel. 1995. "Who Will Vote for You and Why: Designing Strategy and Theme." In James A. Thurber and Candice J. Nelson, eds., *Campaigns and Elections: American Style.* Boulder, Colo.: Westview Press.

Brody, Richard, and Lee Sigelman. 1983. "Presidential Popularity and Presidential Elections: An Update and Extension." *Public Opinion Quarterly* 47 (3): 325–28.

Caddell, Patrick H. 1981. "The Democratic Strategy and Its Electoral Consequences." In Seymour Martin Lipset, ed., *Party Coalitions in the 1980s.* San Francisco: Institute for Contemporary Studies.

Campbell, James E., and Thomas E. Mann. 1992. "Forecasting the 1992 Presidential Election: A User's Guide to the Models." *Brookings Review* 10 (4): 22–27.

Erickson, Robert S. 1989. "Economic Conditions and the Presidential Vote." *American Political Science Review* 83 (June): 567–73.

Finkel, Steven. 1993. "Reexamining the 'Minimal Effects' Model in Recent Presidential Campaigns." *Journal of Politics* 55 (February): 1–21.

Fiorina, Morris P. 1981. *Retrospective Voting in American National Elections.* Yale University Press.

Gelman, Andrew, and Gary King. 1993. "Why Are American Presidential Election Campaign Polls So Variable When Votes Are So Predictable?" *British Journal of Political Science* 23 (4): 409–51.

Greene, Jay P. 1993. "Forewarned before Forecast: Presidential Elections, Forecasting Models, and the 1992 Election." *Political Science and Politics* 26 (1): 17–23.

Herrnson, Paul S. 1988. *Party Campaigning in the 1980s*. Harvard University Press.

———. 1992. "Campaign Professionalism and Fundraising in Congressional Elections." *Journal of Politics* 54 (August): 859–70.

———. 2000. "Hired Guns and House Races: Campaign Professionals in House Elections." In James A. Thurber and Candice J. Nelson, eds., *Campaign Warriors: The Role of Political Consultants in Elections*. Brookings.

Hershey, Margaret. 1989. "The Campaign and the Media." In Gerald M. Pomper, ed., *The Elections of 1988*. Chatham, N.J.: Chatham Publishers.

Hibbs, Douglas A., Jr. 1987. *The American Political Economy: Macroeconomics and Electoral Politics*. Harvard University Press.

Holbrook, Thomas M. 1996. *Do Campaigns Matter?* Thousand Oaks, Calif.: Sage Publications.

Huckfeldt, Robert, and John Sprague. 1992. "Political Parties and Electoral Mobilization: Political Structure, Social Structure, and the Party Canvass." *American Political Science Review* 86 (March): 70–86.

Iyengar, Shanto. 1996. "The Case of the Vanishing Footprints: A Review of Research on Political Campaigns." Paper presented at the annual meeting of the Association for Education in Journalism and Mass Communication, August, Anaheim, Calif..

Iyengar, Shanto, and Nicholas Valentino. Forthcoming. "Who Says What? Source Credibility as a Mediator of Campaign Advertising." In Arthur Lupia and Matthew D. McCubbins, eds., *Elements of Reason*. Cambridge University Press.

Jacobson, Gary C. 1992. *The Politics of Congressional Elections*. Harper Collins.

Keith, Bruce E., David B. Magleby, Candice J. Nelson, Elizabeth Orr, Mark C. Westlye, and Raymond E. Wolfinger. 1992. *The Myth of the Independent Voter*. University of California Press.

Kelley, Stanley, Jr., and Thad W. Mirer. 1974. "The Simple Act of Voting." *American Political Science Review* 68 (June): 572–91.

Key, V. O. 1966. *The Responsible Electorate*. Vintage Books.

Kinder, Donald R. 1997. "Opinion and Action in the Realm of Politics." In Daniel T. Gilbert, Susan T. Fiske, and Gardner Lindzey, eds., *Handbook of Social Psychology*. McGraw-Hill.

Lazarsfeld, Paul, Bernard Berelson, and Hazel Gaudet. 1944. *The People's Choice*. Columbia University Press.

Lewis-Beck, Michael S., and Tom W. Rice. 1992. *Forecasting Elections*. Washington, D.C.: Congressional Quarterly Press.

Markus, Gregory B. 1988. "The Impact of Personal and National Economic Conditions on the Presidential Vote: A Pooled Cross-Sectional Analysis." *American Journal of Political Science* 32 (February): 137–54.

Medvic, Stephen K. 2000. "Professionalization in Congressional Campaigns." In James A. Thurber and Candice J. Nelson, eds., *Campaign Warriors: The Role of Political Consultants in Elections*. Brookings.

Medvic, Stephen K., and Silvio Lenart. 1997. "The Influence of Political Consultants in the 1992 Congressional Elections." *Legislative Studies Quarterly* 22 (1): 61–77.

Petrocik, John. 1989. "An Expected Party Vote: Some New Data for an Old Concept, with Applications." *American Journal of Political Science* 33 (February): 44–66.

———. 1996. "Issue Ownership on Presidential Elections with a 1980 Case Study." *American Journal of Political Science* 40 (August): 825–50.

Petrocik, John, and Frederick T. Steeper. 1989. "Wedges and Magnets: Issues and the Republican Coalition in 1988." *Election Politics* 6: 2–5.

Pfau, Michael, and Henry C. Kensky. 1990. *Attack Politics: Strategy and Defense*. Praeger-Greenwood.

Price, Vincent, and John Zaller. 1993. "Who Gets the News?" *Public Opinion Quarterly* 57 (Summer): 133–64.

Rosenstone, Steven J. 1983. *Forecasting Presidential Elections*. Yale University Press.

Shaw, Daron R. 1999. "The Effect of TV Ads and Candidate Appearances on Statewide Presidential Votes, 1988–1996." *American Political Science Review* 93 (2): 345–61.

Simon, Adam. 1998. "The Winning Message." Ph.D. diss., Department of Political Science, University of California, Los Angeles.

Thurber, James A., and Candice J. Nelson, eds. 2000. *Campaign Warriors: The Role of Political Consultants in Elections*. Brookings.

Wattenberg, Martin, and Craig L. Brians. 1996. "Negative Campaign Advertising: Mobilizer or Demobilizer." Unpublished paper. Department of Political Science, University of California, Irvine.

Wirthlin, Richard B. 1981. "The Republican Strategy and Its Electoral Consequences." In Seymour Martin Lipset, ed., *Party Coalitions in the 1980s*. San Francisco: Institute for Contemporary Studies.

Zaller, John. 1998. "Monica Lewinsky's Contribution to Political Science." *PS: Political Science and Politics* 31 (2): 182–89.

CHAPTER SEVEN

How Issue Ads Have Reshaped American Politics

DARRELL M. WEST

IN 1992 A "PRO-FAMILY" lobbying organization known as the Christian Action Network (CAN) became more and more upset about the liberal drift of social policy in the United States. Led by an activist named Martin Mawyer, the group decided to take action. Too long, it felt, conservatives had sat on the sidelines while the country went downhill. What troubled group members the most was the "gay rights" political agenda that had emerged in preceding decades. A variety of people were devoting themselves to an agenda that, in the eyes of Mawyer, included (1) job quotas for homosexuals, (2) special civil rights laws for homosexuals, and (3) the allowance of homosexuals in the U.S. armed forces. None of these constituted good policy, according to the advocacy organization.

Most galling, though, were the specific efforts that Governor Bill Clinton, then the Democratic candidate for president, was making to appeal to homosexuals and lesbians. Convinced that it was time to take a stand, CAN decided to inform the voting public about Clinton's support for a gay rights agenda. The organization put together a fall television ad entitled "Clinton's Vision for a Better America" that was broadcast at least 250 times in twenty-four major cities across the country right before the election. Along with direct mail letters, op-ed columns, and newspaper advertisements, this commercial condemned Clinton and his running mate Al Gore for supporting radical homosexual rights. Featuring images of the two Democratic candidates in sequence with pictures of young men wearing chains and leather marching in a Gay Pride parade, the ad con-

149

cluded by asking "Is this your vision for a better America?" and providing an address where viewers could write for more information.

The group's $2 million in expenditures that year were not publicly disclosed because the group did not register as a political action committee. Technically, the group considered itself a lobbying organization, not one that advocated the defeat of a particular candidate. The extent of the "public education" campaign came to light only after the Federal Election Commission (FEC) sued CAN for failure to register as a political action committee. However, a federal court judge in Virginia threw out the case as an unconstitutional infringement on the first amendment right to free speech.[1]

In moving from direct lobbying of public officials to public education campaigns, CAN typified a new type of interest group lobbying strategy that has arisen in recent years. The kind of issue advertisement broadcast that year now has become a common sight in American politics. Just witness the following examples of interest group activity:

— In 1998 a California congressional special election won by Lois Capps featured several hundred thousand dollars in issue ads from groups interested in term limits, abortion, and the environment.[2]

— In 1996 the AFL-CIO (American Federation of Labor and Congress of Industrial Organizations) spent $22 million on public education ads (and $35 million overall) in targeted efforts to publicize the health, education, and labor voting records of three dozen House Republicans, mostly freshmen.

— During the 1996 campaign, conservative nonprofit organizations, such as Americans for Tax Reform and the National Right to Life Committee, received more than $4 million from the Republican National Committee in order to organize last-minute mailings, phone calls, and ads right before the election, all outside the scrutiny of campaign finance rules.[3]

— On issues from tobacco reform and health care to tort reform and telecommunications, interest groups have spent extraordinary amounts on advertising, public relations, and grassroots lobbying in order to sway the policy process.

For observers of the political process, the question arising from these contemporary cases is what all this issue advocacy means for American

1. I was an expert witness in this case on the side of the Federal Election Commission.
2. See Gill (1998).
3. Jill Abramson and Leslie Wayne, "Nonprofit Groups Were Partners to Both Parties in Last Election," *New York Times*, October 24, 1997, p. A1; Leslie Wayne, "Papers Detail G.O.P. Ties to Tax Group," *New York Times*, November 10, 1997, p. A27.

democracy. Is this new group activism the flowering of representative democracy or a fundamental threat to the integrity of our system? Are secretive group interests overwhelming the political system and dominating public policymaking?

In this chapter, I argue that issue advocacy campaigns raise a host of problems, both for research and for representative democracy. From the academic standpoint, issue ads raise challenges about how to disentangle the impact of issue ads versus all of the other paid and unpaid communications that appear in election campaigns. Increasingly, ads by candidates are competing with party advertisements, interest group commercials, news, debates, talk radio, and the Internet. As a result of the fragmentation of the campaign media message, it has become more difficult to measure and interpret the impact of ads.

In addition, at the normative level, funding for such campaigns often is generated in secret, far from the disclosure required of other electoral and lobbying tactics. Unlike the advertisements of candidates, who must disclose their spending and contributors, interest groups face no mandatory disclosure as long as they stick to the general goal of public education in their ads. The secrecy inherent in most issue ad campaigns and the fact that such efforts require large amounts of money skew American politics in favor of the well-organized and wealthy, threatening the very foundations of representative government.

In this chapter, I discuss three approaches to reform in this area: doing nothing, increasing disclosure, and regulating issue ads. Given current court rulings equating political spending with freedom of speech, it is very difficult to address the normative problems raised by issue ads. Federal courts effectively have foreclosed many avenues of disclosure and regulation by saying that campaign ads are those that directly use words such as "vote for," "vote against," "elect," or "defeat" a specific candidate. Until judges come to realize the many ways in which candidates, political parties, and interest groups seek to alter voter impressions without using any of these so-called magic words, issue ads will continue to be a major problem for American democracy.

The Rise of Issue Advocacy

Issue advocacy refers to communications whose major purpose is to promote a set of ideas, not particular candidates. For example, the well-publicized 1996 AFL-CIO ads criticizing Republican legislators fell within the realm of issue advocacy because they were "public education" campaigns designed to publicize the voting record of members of Congress. So did the CAN ad decrying radical homosexual rights. Each of these commercials was careful not to cross the line demarked by federal courts of directly exhorting viewers to vote for or against a particular legislator.

Despite the recent proliferation of such ads, issue advocacy is not a new phenomenon. More than eighty years ago, Senator Charles Thomas decried ads by the sugar lobby that appeared during congressional tariff deliberations.[4] Commercials run in 1936 during "The Ford Sunday Evening Hour" bitterly protested Franklin Delano Roosevelt's proposal to establish a social security system. In 1950 the American Medical Association fought against President Harry Truman's health care plan by running ads in 10,000 newspapers, 30 national magazines, and 1,000 radio stations.

More recently, Mobil attracted attention when it ran issue advocacy ads against President Jimmy Carter's energy program. Ten years ago, the nuclear power industry developed a $30 million television ad barrage against proposed restrictions. Beginning in 1992, right-to-life organizations broadcast ads emphasizing the sanctity of life and offering approaches other than abortion to unwanted pregnancies. The acrimonious 1993 debate over the ratification of the North American Free Trade Agreement generated extensive advertising campaigns from competing forces.

What started as a trickle of ads over the past several decades has become a torrent on almost every conceivable topic. In the past few years, groups interested in anti-tobacco legislation, health care, tort reform, term limits, global warming, and a balanced budget have filled the airwaves with commercials promoting their point of view. Once the exception more than the rule, television ads have become the latest form of political volleyball on policy issues.

One reason why issue advocacy has expanded is that interest groups have learned how to evade campaign finance disclosure laws. According to current FEC rules and court decisions, unless groups run ads or produce material that expressly advocates "vote for" or "vote against" Representative Smith, they are not required to register as a political action committee. Emboldened by the failure of the FEC lawsuit against CAN, a wide variety of liberal and conservative interests spanning the political spectrum have used this "public education" loophole to influence the political dialogue without any disclosure of their efforts.

4. Cited in Tom Konda, "Ads on Issues Go Back Decades [Letter to the Editor]," *New York Times*, November 1, 1993, p. A22. Also see Konda (1983).

Recognizing that the post-Watergate system of campaign rules had been gutted, the AFL-CIO announced early in the 1996 presidential campaign that it would spend $35 million running ads in the districts of Republican members of Congress who opposed labor objectives. Even though these ads would be broadcast in the run-up to the election and would mention the names of the Republican representatives along with unfavorable commentary on their voting patterns, the AFL-CIO declared these expenditures as issue advocacy and therefore not subject to federal disclosure rules. In response, the Coalition, a consortium of thirty-five business groups including the U.S. Chamber of Commerce, National Restaurant Association, and National Association of Manufacturers, said it would raise $17 million on a pro-business advocacy campaign defending these Republican incumbents. Although the group ultimately fell far short of its fundraising target, its ads were not subject to federal campaign laws because they too fell under the guise of public education as opposed to electoral advocacy.

Figures for issue advocacy overall are difficult to estimate because public disclosure of such efforts is not required owing to their official status as "non-campaign" activities. However, a comprehensive report by the Annenberg Public Policy Center of the University of Pennsylvania estimated that in 1995 and 1996 somewhere between $135 million and $150 million was spent on issue advocacy advertising by at least thirty-one groups, including the $35 million spent by labor. This was about one-third of the total of $400 million spent on advertising by candidates in federal races in that election cycle.[5]

The chief virtue of public advocacy ads is that groups are able to frame policy battles and develop narratives in ways that favor themselves. Unlike interview shows and the news, which are controlled by journalists, ads are controlled by the sponsoring interest group. Interest groups understand that ads are the most reliable means of conveying political messages because groups control the content and timing of the message. Television appeals allow them to present unmediated messages directly to the viewing public.

Reliance on the news to fight symbolic policy battles is risky because reporters are professional skeptics who cannot be counted on to convey a group's perspective. Authors from Thomas Patterson to James Fallows have noted how cynical journalists have become in the contemporary period and how this deeply rooted skepticism skews press coverage in a

5. Beck et al. (1997).

direction that exudes suspicions about any organization.[6] In this situation, it makes more sense for interested groups to dictate their messages directly as opposed to communicating through the intermediary of news reporters.

Timing is everything in politics. Groups in the middle of political battles need to make strategic moves on the turn of a dime. Getting a reporter to write a favorable story a week too late will not advance the group's interests. Organizations require timeliness and repetition in their political messages in order to enhance effectiveness. Moreover, news coverage is usually a one-time occurrence, which often has modest impact. Paid advertising allows repetition of a message, which enhances its effect.

Despite—or perhaps because of—their proliferation, many policy advocacy campaigns do not succeed. In the area of abortion, for example, the news coverage that followed the airing of pro-life commercials was neither extensive nor favorable to the groups running the ads. The press characterized the sponsors of these commercials as self-interested and politically suspect, both fatal flaws in shaping public opinion.[7]

The ineffectiveness of much past advocacy advertising has led to the view that these types of ads will never be influential. Interest groups that run ads have clearly partisan objectives and therefore are not seen as credible by reporters, legislators, or the public. Furthermore, policy advertising is tricky because of its multiple audiences—opinion leaders, elected officials, grassroots activists, and the general public, each of whom may respond differently to the same ad. Few interest groups have sufficient financial resources to be taken seriously in advocacy advertising. In general, the amount of money spent on policy advertising pales in comparison to the $30 million to $40 million that each candidate, on average, spent on ads in recent presidential general elections or the $500 million that IBM spends annually to market its products. Yet as documented by West and Loomis, several recent advocacy campaigns on tobacco, health care, and telecommunications have yielded important victories for private sector groups.[8]

The Challenge for Researchers

With the large amounts of money going into issue advocacy, two questions arising for researchers are whether and under what conditions issue

---

6. Patterson (1994); Fallows (1996).
7. West (1988).
8. West and Loomis (1998).

ads are effective and what quality of information is presented to voters? Researchers typically have devoted far greater effort to understanding the power of candidate ads than issue ads. The reasons for this focus are clear. Most paid campaign messages in the past were run by candidates, not outside interest groups.

However, in recent years, the balance has shifted between candidate and other ads in political campaigns. In 1996, for example, 26 percent ($140 million) of all advertising messages ($540 million) came from issue ads. Groups such as U.S. Term Limits, the Sierra Club, the AFL-CIO, groups of business organizations, Americans for Tax Reform, and the National Right to Life Committee, among others, spent millions "educating" the American public about pet causes. In 1998 nearly 40 percent of all advertisements aired in the few months leading up to the election came from groups and parties, not candidates.

The rise in the proportion of campaign messages emanating from private interest groups is creating great difficulties for researchers who study ads. The old problem in the area of political communications was in separating the impact of ads from news. To what degree did paid spots, in contrast to newspaper coverage, television broadcasts, and radio shows, affect how people saw the candidates?

With the fragmentation of the campaign media message into lots of different components—candidate ads, party spots, independent expenditures, issue advocacy, newspapers, television news, talk radio, and the Internet—massive measurement and conceptual problems arise in disentangling the impact of various sources of information. If ads influence citizens, does it matter if the ad is run by the candidate, a political party, or a small interest group? Given the different roles that candidates, parties, and groups play in American politics, it is likely that the source of the ad matters a lot to how researchers evaluate the impact of ads in contemporary campaigns. Ads sponsored by narrow interest groups, for example, pose different challenges for democracy than ads run by candidates or broad-based political parties.

In addition, research on the 1998 campaign reveals that appeals broadcast by political parties and interest groups are more likely to contain negative and misleading information and to be less specific about the issues.[9] Since accurate and informative material is vital for voters seeking to evaluate the candidates, these so-called issue ads bring into question the

9. Alliance for Better Campaigns (1998/99), p. 3. Also see West (forthcoming).

quality of the information that appears before voters. Indeed, it suggests that issue ads should be renamed nonissue ads!

The Challenge for Representative Democracy

Beyond the question of how to measure what moves the needle, the rise of issue advocacy raises a number of normative problems for representative government. One is the high degree of secrecy that accompanies such campaigns. Increasingly, public advocacy is being supplemented by "stealth" campaigns in which direct disclosure of lobbying activities is masked from the public through "fronts" or alliances with other organizations. For example, Covington and Burling, the law firm representing the major tobacco companies (Philip Morris, R. J. Reynolds, Lorillard, and Brown and Williamson) privately spent $1 million of Philip Morris money to finance an international magazine called *Healthy Buildings*, which used suspect science to promote the industry's claim that bans on indoor smoking were unnecessary.[10] In 1996 the firm also commissioned a study arguing that proposed federal tobacco restrictions would cost the nation 92,000 jobs and $7.9 billion in lost output.

Stealth campaigns have spread to election campaigns. Larry Sabato and Glenn Simpson report in their book *Dirty Little Secrets* how interests use secret means to plant negative information with voters.[11] One such technique has been so-called "push polls," in which mock pollsters call thousands of voters to ask whether their vote would be altered if they knew something negative about the candidate. In a Wisconsin congressional district, for example, push polls secretly were employed to accuse a female candidate of being a lesbian.

These and other promotional activities illustrate the wide range of stealth campaigns being conducted today. Stealth lobbying can take many forms, from event sponsorship to commissioned think tank research projects to public opinion polls that get leaked to the press. Some groups work with so-called 501(c)(3) tax-exempt organizations. These alliances offer the advantage of freedom from any required disclosure as well as tax deductibility of group contributions.[12] The particular form can vary, but the key

10. Sheila Kaplan, "Tobacco Dole," *Mother Jones Magazine*, August 4, 1997, www.ctyme.com/dole/tobacco.htm.
11. Sabato and Simpson (1996).
12. Eliza Newlin Carney, "Stealth Bombers," *National Journal*, August 16, 1997, pp. 1640–43.

in each of these efforts is that the actual sponsor is masked by front organizations that make it difficult for the public to see who really is funding the activity.

Stealth campaigns consciously are designed to fly under the radar of press and public oversight. Unpopular interests recognize that one of the most important aspects of effective communications is "source credibility." Individuals or groups that are seen by the public as being independent or unbiased are more persuasive than those that are not. Interests that lack source credibility hide their activities under innocuous-sounding alliances, such as the National Smokers Alliance or Citizens for a Sound Economy. The former is funded directly by Philip Morris, while the latter is a conservative group devoted to lessening government regulation of the private sector.

From the standpoint of the affected interest, these alliances can be extremely effective. Companies that run ads or sponsor activities addressing policy controversies do not have to reveal their direct support. Rather, the company can hide behind the alliance and shield itself from public suspicions about its motives for staking out a particular policy stance. This enables the company to avoid whatever backlash arises when the public or the press realizes who actually is sponsoring the event in question.

At the same time, such activities help private interests to evade public disclosure rules governing lobbying and campaigning. According to federal rules, groups that lobby Congress or contribute directly to candidates for office are required to disclose the date and amount of the contribution. This information is released periodically to the press and general public. If, however, the group labels its activities as public education, public disclosure is not required of the contributors or expenditures. The group can spend millions of dollars influencing the public without being accountable for their efforts. For "pariah" interests or unpopular causes, such as tobacco companies, it is the ideal form of political advocacy.

In addition to the problem of secrecy, difficulties arise from issue advocacy relating to political power. Traditionally, the many countervailing forces present in American politics have been seen as limiting the power of particular interests and lobbying efforts. Narrow interest groups can be outvoted at election time by the general public. Political parties, social movements, and public interest groups can speak for larger segments of society than do particularistic groups.

However, in light of contemporary developments in the area of issue advocacy, it is time to reexamine the efficacy of voters, political parties, and social movements in limiting the power of well-organized and well-financed interests, especially as these interests have become more and more skillful at shaping the presentation of their favored issues. In an era where moneyed interests are able to convey their messages ad nauseam, in any number of ways, many forces that historically have protected general interests may have lost their impact.

The ultimate countervailing force in American democracy is the electorate. Voters are more numerous and more diverse than the membership of any specialized interest. Even the largest interest group in America (the American Association of Retired Persons, with 33 million members) includes a modest percentage of the overall electorate. Labor unions as a whole represent about 14 percent of the work force. This proportion pales in comparison to the percentage of American citizens (half in 1996) who vote in presidential elections.

Because they are taxpayers and members of multiple groups, voters as a whole are more likely than interest groups to represent collective interests. Voters pay the cost of government programs, and they foot the bill for special tax breaks or subsidies granted to interest groups. The fact that group success in taxing the public till comes at the expense of the broad electorate gives voters clear incentives to serve as a check on group power.

If special interests ask too much of government or win too many public benefits, according to classical group theorists as well as founders like James Madison, this will threaten the interests of the general public and mobilize citizens to prevent greedy raids on the federal treasury. In *The Governmental Process*, David Truman argued that the dynamics of interest group mobilization limit the demands that private organizations place on government.[13] An inordinate amount of success on the part of some groups inevitably fosters a counter-mobilization by other groups. When excessive group demands lead to burgeoning government spending, anti-spending groups emerge to fight for taxpayer rights.

As with the textbook lobbying model, it is not clear that the large mass of unorganized voters can countervail well-organized special interests. The costs of organizing typically outweigh the diffuse social benefits gained.[14] As a general entity, the public is notoriously difficult to organize. People have diverse interests, and many do not care about politics. In an era of massive public cynicism about politicians, it is difficult for the public to

13. Truman (1951).
14. Olson (1965).

get outraged about particular pieces of legislation. Sweetheart deals are just "more of the same" for many ordinary people.

In the absence of a clear consensus on social action, voters must search out information and decide which course of action best protects themselves. Issue advocacy campaigns provide such material, but from a clear and oftentimes secret point of view. The difficulty that ordinary people have in gathering information relevant to their self-interest restricts the public's ability to win out over smaller but better organized interests. The result is that citizens have lost some of their electoral power to protect their overall interests and restrain the power of parochial interest groups.

Because of the difficulty of organizing the general public, political parties historically have been seen as the most effective way for broad coalitions of interests to countervail the power of special interest groups. The broad-based nature of political parties and the fact that they must compete for government seats before the general public give parties special advantages in terms of political mobilization.[15]

Due to their influential role in policymaking, parties have an advantage over the citizenry in shaping the public dialogue. Simply by dint of their more broad-based coalitions, parties force interest groups to negotiate their differences. The need to win victories when voters have a direct say encourages parties to restrain group demands.

But parties have difficulty representing general social interests. The traditional argument that the breadth of party coalitions restrains factions within the party is undermined by contemporary realities. Labor unions and trial lawyers have been particularly powerful in the Democratic party, while small business, fundamentalists, and corporations are well-represented in the Republican party.

This fragmentation of party coalitions has generated fear that parties have been captured by special interests. If parties are dependent on private money to finance elections and issue advocacy campaigns, their ability to contravene specialized interests is reduced. Since the costs of electioneering have risen at a much faster clip than overall inflation, parties have intensified their fundraising efforts. The 1997 congressional hearings into campaign finance abuses, for example, publicized dozens of ways in which moneyed interests curried favor with political parties through financial contributions. This dependency has limited the ability of parties to stand

15. Sundquist (1983).

above specialized interests and, in the eyes of some, has undermined the historic role of parties in countervailing interest groups.

Parties represent the views of those who are active politically, but who represents the disenfranchised? One of the problems of political systems is representing those who lack resources and do not participate politically. By the nature of electoral imperatives, politicians are especially attuned to the interests of those who directly control their fate. In Democratic elections where large sums of cash are required for electioneering activities, this means voters and contributors. But because voters are poorly organized and half do not even bother to vote, legislators often pay closer attention to their contributors than their constituents.

From a systemic standpoint, this produces a situation where large numbers of citizens feel that their interests are poorly represented. This occurs because politicians pay far less attention to the politically weak and disadvantaged. These segments of society are poorly organized, do not run issue ads, and vote less frequently than those with higher levels of income and education.

It used to be that, with modest resources, social movements could win influence through rallies, protests, and demonstrations. Each of these strategies of mobilization required a considerable amount of time and effort, but not too much in the way of financial resources. Community organizers would merely spend time pointing out to people how their interests were being abused and over the course of time would build a movement out of the disenfranchised.

But political protest in a high-tech era is much more problematic. As tools of issue advocacy require more access to financial resources, it is more difficult to mobilize and represent the disenfranchised. Minority groups, citizens associations, and public interest organizations do not have money for television ads, direct mail, phone banks, or Internet sites. This puts them at a serious disadvantage when lobbying requires access to resources. Even Ross Perot, who has invested nearly $100 million of his own money in support of his populist cause, has, with the exception of deficit reduction, made little impact on the national political landscape.

As lobbying has come to center on expensive communications technologies, the voices of the disadvantaged and unorganized have become even less a part of the policy discourse. It requires money and organization to participate in contemporary political battles. This skews political mobilization away from community activists and toward media consultants, public relations experts, and direct mail specialists.

What Needs to Be Done?

There are three major options for dealing with the problems raised by issue advocacy in American politics: do nothing, broaden disclosure, or increase regulation. Each approach diagnoses the problem differently and calls for different kinds of remedies. Let me review the logic behind each in turn.

Do Nothing

One prominent line of thinking—blending Senator Mitch McConnell (R-Ky.) with the American Civil Liberties Union (ACLU)—assumes that nothing seriously is broken in American politics and that therefore nothing dramatic needs to be done. Among the advocates for this view are some surprising allies, such as the Republican National Committee, the Sierra Club, and the ACLU. Uniting these organizations is the view that the first amendment right to freedom of speech trumps all attempts at regulation and most ambitious efforts at disclosure.

In the court case *Federal Election Commission* v. *Christian Action Network, Inc., and Martin Mawyer,* which dealt with issue advocacy in the 1992 presidential campaign, the ACLU of Virginia took a near-absolutist line on federal regulation of public education campaigns. Even though CAN had run a television ad just before the 1992 general election featuring pictures of candidates Bill Clinton and Al Gore and had attacked their stance in favor of homosexual rights, the ACLU urged District Judge James C. Turk in an amicus curiae brief not to interpret the ad as expressly advocating the defeat of Clinton and Gore. Such a decision, the ACLU argued, would infringe on freedom of speech. "One incursion into inferential interpretation of speech content will lead rapidly to another," the ACLU gravely predicted.[16] Taking note of the possible danger, Judge Turk threw the case out before it ever was tried on grounds the FEC had exceeded the limit of the First Amendment.

But what such logic ignores is the danger of one-sided group advocacy in the free exchange of ideas. The Fourteenth Amendment to the U.S. Constitution guarantees equal protection under the law. Indeed, the provision has been widely used to extend equal protection in the areas of civil rights, pay equity, and voting rights, among other areas. Despite the cen-

16. Amicus curiae brief of ACLU filed in the Fourth Circuit, U.S. Court of Appeals, Docket 95-2600, filed January 22, 1996.

trality of political communications, courts have failed to see any danger to freedom of speech from one-sided advocacy. If one set of interests has the money to broadcast an ad while others do not, it represents a serious challenge to the ensuing discourse. There can be little robust exchange of views if only one side has the resources required for policy advocacy.

Broaden Disclosure

A second approach defines the situation very differently. Rather than seeing no malady, this perspective diagnoses the money in politics as a serious problem with a specific remedy: greater disclosure on the part of interest groups. In a media environment, money is central to the public contesting of political ideas, and thus more openness and less secrecy are the essential first steps in establishing minimally equitable grounds for civic discourse.

The logic behind this idea undergirds current reforms on lobbying and campaign finance. Individuals or groups who give money directly to elected officials or their campaign funds must disclose the nature of the gift, its amount, and when the contribution was made. For decades, this type of disclosure has been the bedrock of anti corruption efforts. Since the turn of the century, when bribes and cash payoffs were routine parts of American politics, reformers have argued that outright gifts need not be outlawed, but must be disclosed so that people can see for themselves who is lobbying Congress and financing campaign efforts.

Over time, past reforms and old rules have been attacked by legions of lawyers and consultants, whose job it is to create loopholes and craft new means of influencing politics outside the disclosure requirements. For example, ads that advocate the election or defeat of federal candidates for office must have, on-screen or on-air, a short disclosure message indicating who paid for the ad. That way, viewers have some chance to determine for themselves who paid for the ads and to evaluate this source of information.

Unfortunately, the text or voice-overs identifying the sponsor of an ad are on the screen for just five seconds, which is not long enough for many viewers to identify the ad's sponsor. In one study of the 1996 elections, only half of the participants in focus groups were able to identify the sponsors of campaign ads they had just seen. In one spot, that of an independent ad on retirement savings accounts broadcast by the American Council of Life Insurance, only 40 percent correctly identified its sponsor. Of the remaining viewers, 20 percent erroneously believed it was paid for by the

Clinton campaign, 20 percent did not know who broadcast the ad, and 20 percent incorrectly believed it was sponsored by the Cato Institute because that organization had been listed on-screen at the beginning of the spot as the footnote for a claim made during the commercials.[17] Moreover, many advocacy ads list sponsors whose names give viewers or reporters no clue as to their actual stake in the advertisement.

At a minimum, effective disclosure of advertising sponsors is a first step in allowing for reasoned public discourse. Rather than having disclosure text be on-screen for only five seconds, the sponsorship should be shown continuously throughout the ad's presentation. Viewers could better determine which organization is sponsoring the ad and be in a stronger position to evaluate its content.

Recent policy battles have seen the rise of issue advocacy ads, independent expenditures, and stealth campaigns, all with little required disclosure. Indeed, the last decade has seen an explosion of spending on so-called public education campaigns. This can take the form either of communications about a candidate running for office or a piece of legislation currently before Congress.

The rise of issue advocacy and stealth campaigns surely suggests that current disclosure rules should be tightened. There should be more timely and complete disclosure of independent expenditures and issue advocacy in election campaigns. For example, ads that show pictures or discuss stances of specific candidates in the sixty days before an election should be treated as campaign ads and be subject to current federal rules on campaign expenditures, including the disclosure of contributors.

Communications that address legislation currently before Congress should comply with federal lobbying rules. This means that the amount and timing of such expenditures need to be reported publicly so that reporters and the public can see who is trying to influence the policy process. Current rules have become very strict for disclosing inside lobbying activities, such as gifts, but completely lax for disclosing outside or stealth lobbying. Only by revealing the contributions and spending involved in such efforts can there be accountability for the new forms of lobbying that have arisen in recent years. Otherwise, as witnessed by *Roll Call* ads and CNN (Cable News Network) time buys, interests that can afford it will dominate the framing of many issues.

17. West (1997).

Disclosure reforms receive strong support from the American public. According to a 1996 national survey, 76 percent of Americans believe that interest groups running public education campaigns about the issues should disclose who is paying for the ad, and 74 percent also believe that these groups should be subject to the same campaign finance rules as candidates.[18]

The idea behind broadening disclosure does not imply that such lobbying should be regulated. In and of itself, disclosure does not restrict freedom of expression or threaten the free exchange of political ideas. Rather, effective, timely disclosure helps to protect democracy. Once group efforts are made public, voters can judge for themselves whether a particular lobbying activity is worthy of consideration.

Increase Regulation

A third perspective defines the problem of money and politics as fundamental in a democracy and therefore proposes the most substantial type of response—direct regulation of group advocacy. Although disclosure is seen as laudatory, it simply will not go far enough in protecting public discourse. The threat of secret advocacy and domination by wealthy interests has grown so problematic from this point of view that more rigorous regulations need to be put into effect, ironically to *protect* freedom of expression.

One such area where regulation is needed is in the rules restricting the most insidious types of stealth activities being conducted today, both in campaigns and in lobbying. Electronic smear campaigns have become a key by-product of new communications technologies and typically are filled with misleading, erroneous, or outright malicious claims.

Recognizing the danger that such expressions have for Democratic systems, a number of states have either considered or actually passed "truth in communications" codes. In subscribing to such a code, candidates for office (or lobbying groups and organizations) agree not to distribute fraudulent, forged, or falsely identified writing, agree to approve personally all literature or advertising for their campaign, and agree to retract or correct immediately any claim discovered to be inaccurate.

For example, a Connecticut bill that would have adopted such a code passed in the state house of representatives. Kentucky has a bill pending that would ban ads using "false, deceptive, or misleading" statements.

18. West (1997).

New Jersey considered but rejected a truth-in-campaign act that would have created a commission to investigate complaints about ads alleged to contain "any false statement of material fact." The penalty would have been $5,000 for the first offense and $10,000 for each subsequent offense.

In an effort to deal with independent expenditures, South Dakota considered but did not pass a similar bill requiring individuals who run ads mentioning a candidate at least ten days before an election to provide a copy of the ad to that candidate. Some states have developed rules aimed at media consultants. In Michigan, for example, a bill passed the state senate that would have fined consultants up to $1,000 for producing ads in violation of disclosure laws.

A few states have passed rules regulating the content of ads and other types of political communications. Montana has a statute making it unlawful for a person to make a "false statement" about a candidate's public voting record or to make a "false statement" that reflects unfavorably on a candidate's character or morality. North Dakota bans statements that are "untrue, deceptive, or misleading." Oregon has a statute banning ads with "false statements." Unlike other states, this law also has a significant penalty: "If the finder of fact finds by clear and convincing evidence that the false statement of fact reversed the outcome of the election, the defendant shall be deprived of the nomination or election." Washington requires the pictures of candidates used in ads to be no less than five years old. Political ads also must not contain a "false statement of material fact."

More detailed guidelines come from the National Fair Campaign Practices Committee, an industry organization made up of political consultants and practitioners. According to its code of fair campaign practices, candidates for public office have an obligation to uphold basic principles of decency, honesty, and fair play. This includes condemnation of personal vilification and avoidance of character defamation, whispering campaigns, libel, slander, or scurrilous attacks.

The code condemns the use of political material that misrepresents, distorts, or otherwise falsifies the facts regarding any candidate as well as malicious or unfounded accusations aimed at creating doubts as to loyalty and patriotism. Appeals to prejudice based on race, creed, sex, or national origin are to be avoided. Candidates are asked to repudiate any individuals or groups that resort to improper methods or tactics. Anyone who believes that these rules have been violated can file a complaint with the committee that gets publicized in the industry. Nine states (California, Hawaii, Illinois, Kansas, Maine, Montana, Nevada, Washington, and West

Virginia) have statutes modeled after the National Fair Campaign Practices Committee code.

In recent years, Wisconsin has adopted the most sweeping regulation of issue advocacy. According to a twenty-two-year-old state law, any groups or persons engaged in activities having "the purpose of influencing the election" must register with the state Elections Board and disclose their donors. Ads or other types of communications may not be paid for with corporate or union money. During the 1996 election, state courts ordered off the air several ads critical of state legislators on grounds that the groups involved, such as Americans for Limited Terms, the Sierra Club, and Wisconsin Manufacturers and Commerce, had not disclosed their contributors.[19]

At the national level, Congressman Ernest Istook Jr. (R-Okla.) sought to deal with issue lobbying from tax-exempt, nonprofit groups by proposing legislation that would oversee such activities. Groups that are federally funded would be required to disclose their lobbying activities to the federal agency awarding the grant. This legislative proposal unleashed a tidal wave of bitter criticism from the affected groups. Groups from the National Right to Life Committee to Planned Parenthood protested what they saw as an effort to "gag" their freedom of expression. Although some Republican leaders initially favored the legislation, the sharp outcry that ensued effectively prevented passage of the amendment.

While Congress has debated what to do in this area, still another federal agency quietly but persistently has stepped up its regulatory oversight of group advocacy. The Internal Revenue Service (IRS) has begun to examine the lobbying and political activities of nonprofit groups with tax-exempt status with an eye toward revoking the tax exemption of groups engaged in blatant political activities. According to federal law, so-called 501(c)(3) organizations must not engage in *any* electioneering activities and must avoid any substantial amount of political lobbying. The IRS goal is not to limit freedom of expression, but to make sure that federal taxpayers do not subsidize lobbying groups under the guise of public charities.

In a prominent audit of an abortion rights organization, the IRS reviewed the group's fundraising letters in order to determine if the group had crossed the line separating charitable from political activities. Finding

19. Amy Keller, "Wisconsin Regulates 'Election-Related' Issue Ads," *Roll Call*, September 4, 1997.

that the group's letters showed a "clear implication" and a "clear preference" for particular candidates, the IRS moved to revoke its tax-exempt
status. When those thresholds are crossed, the IRS pronounced, "voter
education becomes voter direction."[20]

This ruling has been of obvious interest to a wide range of tax-exempt
organizations because of the unmistakable signal that the IRS is cracking
down on blatantly political groups. Overall, right now, the IRS has about
thirty charities under review for excessive political activities. In addition,
there have been other cases, such as one involving the application of the
Christian Coalition for tax-exempt status, that the IRS did not approve
because of concerns over the group's electioneering activities.

Conclusions

At one level, the problem of issue advocacy in politics is almost impossible
to resolve. There are competing reform principles, such as equity, freedom, and representativeness, all of which conflict with one another. It is
possible to pass laws that encourage free political expression, such as raising contributor limits in campaigns, but also aggravate the resource ineq-
uity of American politics. Or it is possible to create new accountability
measures that attempt to regulate the truthfulness of group advocacy and
also dampen freedom of expression.

This does not mean that reform is impossible. There are a number of
formal and informal changes that would improve the public discourse.
For example, journalists must come to terms with their responsibilities for
monitoring the voices of the new heavenly chorus. Groups could and should
receive the same scrutiny reserved for candidates. Stealth campaigns must
be investigated vigorously to see who funds campaigns that are simulta-
neously hidden and public. Alone among major players in the political
system, reporters have the credibility to demand answers to tough questions about group advocacy.

In the absence of other safeguards, the press must work to encourage
coherent discourse and accountability in group conflict. The most egre-
gious lies and misstatements in group advocacy must be exposed, publicized, or, at a minimum, simply ignored. Journalists need to cover public
lobbying, without amplifying questionable claims by self-interested par-

20. Damon Chappie, "The IRS's 'Story of M' May Affect '96 Politics," *Roll Call*, April
15, 1996, p. 1.

ties to a policy dispute. Simply being aware of the pitfalls in press coverage, such as ignoring small organizations or paying disproportionate attention to large ones, would go a long way toward improving the public dialogue.

Interest groups themselves must understand the need for some self-regulation and self-restraint. Democracy has survived in the United States for more than two centuries because of voluntary limits on group conduct and a general agreement to play by widely shared rules of the game. Strangely enough, increased amounts of group activity may not improve the quality of debate, but rather demean it, because interests have great incentives to construct self-interested and parochial stories.

At a minimum, groups must stand for truthfulness in public claims, for tolerance of opposing viewpoints, and against illegal or unethical tactics. Unfettered group competition damages the system in the same way that overgrazing ruins the village commons. As they put forth their arguments, groups must recognize their own role in protecting the overall system in which they operate.

Even with improved press oversight and self-restraint on the part of groups, some legal changes are required to safeguard the contemporary system. Stronger disclosure laws are necessary to ensure a rough fairness of contemporary discourse. In the absence of information on who sponsors expensive ads or mails slick brochures, neither elites, nor reporters, nor the public knows who is behind particular claims or how such communications should be evaluated. Truth and accuracy provisions in mass communications need to be strengthened in order to ensure that discourse is conducted in an honest manner.

References

Alliance for Better Campaigns. 1998/99. "Party Issue Ads Become Weapon of First Resort, Study Finds." *Political Standard* 1 (December/January): 3.

Beck, Deborah, Paul Taylor, Jeffrey Stanger, and Douglas Rivlin. 1997. "Issue Advocacy during the 1996 Campaign." Report by the Annenberg Public Policy Center, University of Pennsylvania, September.

Fallows, James. 1996. *Breaking the News*. Vintage Books.

Gill, Jeff. 1998. "One Year and Four Elections: A Case Study of Campaign Conduct in the 1998 Capps Campaign for California's 22nd District." Paper presented at the conference on Money, Media, and Madness, American University, Center for Congressional and Presidential Studies, Washington, D.C., December.

Konda, Thomas. 1983. *Political Advertising and Public Relations by Business in the United States.* Ph.D. diss., Department of Political Science, University of Kentucky.
Olson, Mancur. 1965. *The Logic of Collective Action.* Harvard University Press.
Patterson, Thomas. 1994. *Out of Order.* Vintage Books.
Sabato, Larry, and Glenn Simpson. 1996. *Dirty Little Secrets.* Times Books.
Sundquist, James. 1983. *The Dynamics of the Party System,* rev. ed. Brookings.
Truman, David. 1951. *The Governmental Process.* Alfred Knopf.
West, Darrell M. 1988. "Activists and Economic Policymaking in Congress." *American Journal of Political Science* 32 (August): 662–80.
———. 1997. *Air Wars: Television Advertising in Election Campaigns, 1952–1996,* 2d ed. Washington, D.C.: Congressional Quarterly Press.
———. Forthcoming. *Checkbook Democracy: How Money Corrupts Political Campaigns.* Northeastern University Press.
West, Darrell M., and Burdett Loomis. 1998. *The Sound of Money: How Political Interests Get What They Want.* Norton.

CHAPTER EIGHT

Summary and Conclusions

DAVID A. DULIO

CANDICE J. NELSON

JAMES A. THURBER

ARE CAMPAIGN TELEVISION ADS good or bad for democracy? What are the effects of contrast and negative advertisements? Do issue ads harm representative democracy? The research reported in this volume addresses these questions and contributes to our knowledge about the role that televised political advertising plays in modern election campaigns. The contributors to this book address important questions that are on the cutting edge of the political advertising field and report on the most recent research. The essays span many of the most important and controversial issues related to the characteristics and consequences of using television ads in campaigns that both scholars and practitioners have been struggling with since the medium became a central part of politics.

The authors address different *types* of televised advertising—from candidate-sponsored advertising and its effects on voters and vote choices to interest group issue advertising and its effects on democracy and pluralism. The essays also span different types of elections that usually employ airborne advertising in modern elections—U.S. House of Representatives (Herrnson and Patterson, chapter 5), U.S. Senate (Kahn and Kenney, chapter 4), and presidential (Jamieson, Waldman, and Sherr, chapter 3; Iyengar and Petrocik, chapter 6). These authors make contributions in at least five areas that will advance the scholarly study of political advertising: theoretical, empirical, methodological, normative, and practical. In this chapter, we discuss the rich mix of these contributions with a special focus on the authors' most important conclusions, many of which stem from the authors' challenges to the conventional wisdom surrounding the study of political advertising. Some of the findings are at odds with campaign myths, practical knowledge, and some of the previous scholarly literature.

What is the impact of negative television advertising? This central research question is posed by Lau and Sigelman in chapter 2, which establishes the framework for many of the other chapters and for the study of television in campaigns. By summarizing past research, Lau and Sigelman provide a baseline from which to contrast the findings of Jamieson, Waldman, and Sherr and of Kahn and Kenney. The theoretical, empirical, and methodological innovations found in chapter 3 are all the more apparent after Lau and Sigelman outline the "traditional" model of advertising. The traditional categorization of ads as positive (advocacy) or negative (attack) is challenged by Jamieson, Waldman, and Sherr, who argue that to this point scholars have been going about their study of advertising incorrectly. Lau and Sigelman also review the debate on the effect of negative ads on voters and find that "there is no strong preponderance of evidence indicating that political attack ads are more memorable than advocacy ads." In their chapter, Kahn and Kenney break from Lau and Sigelman's conclusions and with much of the previous literature to show that voters *do* recall more information after seeing negative advertisements.

In addition to reviewing previous findings, Lau and Sigelman take great care in describing the *methods* that have produced those findings. For example, their review of the methods used by Ansolabehere and Iyengar in their experimental analyses illustrates the advantages of this design for this type of research.[1] Lau and Sigelman contrast experimental analysis with the use of surveys in the context of advertising research and argue that surveys are the "second-best evidence" for this research (especially in studies that test respondents' exposure to and recall of ads). They argue that experiments are more powerful in that they afford researchers the opportunity to control the exposure to the phenomenon under study. Surveys, in contrast, do not provide for such a captive audience and are less lifelike. No study reviewed by Lau and Sigelman employs *both* an experimental and a survey design. Iyengar and Petrocik in chapter 6, however, use both designs to test their hypotheses, lending greater reliability to their results and answering the criticisms outlined by Lau and Sigelman in chapter 2.

Placed in the context of Lau and Sigelman's summary of the empirical literature, the contributions of the other chapters fall into five categories,

---

1. Ansolabehere and Iyengar (1995).

as we see them: theoretical, empirical, methodological, normative, and practical. The research reported in this volume challenges much of the prior work outlined by Lau and Sigelman. There is no greater example than the chapter by Jamieson, Waldman, and Sherr, which takes issue with how previous scholars have defined "negative" advertising. The standard practice, reviewed by Lau and Sigelman, of dichotomizing television advertisements into positive and negative ads is incorrect according to Jamieson and her colleagues. Instead, they argue that research must not ignore the difference between contrast and comparison ads and truly negative ads. Jamieson, Waldman, and Sherr also challenge the existing scheme for measuring the amount of negativity that appears in ads. They move away from the general categorization of ads as either attack or advocacy and develop a measure—the concept of the idea unit—that they argue is more accurate than any existing measure in identifying the information conveyed by an ad to the public. Each idea unit, which is operationalized as a single claim by the candidate in the ad, is coded as either attack or advocacy, which yields the most complete rating of ads in the literature to date. They also urge political scientists to measure the level of attack in an ad by using the technology that is available today for tracking the number of television gross ratings points placed on ads. Doing so would allow researchers to measure accurately the investment in air time and the content of ads that is absorbed by the voters.

These advances in conceptualization and measurement lead directly to Jamieson, Waldman, and Sherr's findings, which, like their methods, run contrary to much of the scholarly literature. The authors argue that if contrast ads are considered in addition to advocacy and attack ads, the amount of actual attack in past ads is much less than has been reported in the literature. However, the more important empirical finding is that attack and contrast ads actually carry more policy information than pure advocacy ads.

The contribution of Jamieson, Waldman, and Sherr is based on a careful accounting of what exactly is contained in television advertisements. Kahn and Kenney's evidence that negative ads are more informative than positive ads, and therefore are more useful to the electorate, reinforces these findings. This evidence breaks from much of the prior research, outlined by Lau and Sigelman, which has shown that negative ads are not any more memorable than positive ads. Kahn and Kenney find that the more negative ads voters viewed, the more likely they were to identify candidates' names, make ideological judgments about them, and recognize campaign themes. The reliability of this research is enhanced by Kahn and Kenney's methodology and multiple tests of their hypotheses.

In another methodological recommendation, Iyengar and Petrocik caution researchers not to rely too much on the National Election Study (NES) surveys that are conducted during the traditional campaign period from Labor Day to election day, after many voters have already formed their choices. In order to examine true voter choice formation, Iyengar and Petrocik argue and illustrate that we must look at voters' decisionmaking prior to Labor Day. Finally, West (chapter 7) challenges researchers to examine issue advocacy campaigns more closely. The difficulties that face researchers—the proliferation of issue advocacy groups and therefore of advertisements as well as the effort involved in tracking their activity— may be mitigated somewhat by the technology discussed by Jamieson, Waldman, and Sherr. The gross rating point data that can be employed to track the amount of time a certain spot airs also can be helpful to researchers interested in issue advocacy. By tracking ads and the groups that sponsor them—candidates, parties, or issue advocacy groups—researchers will be better equipped to answer the challenges posed by West.

Herrnson and Patterson make another empirical and methodological contribution in their use of a unique data set on congressional elections. By merging data from voter exit polls with data from a survey of candidates, Herrnson and Patterson are able to conduct an individual-level analysis like no other in the literature. Their test of the importance of campaign advertising on the election-day outcome, while indirect, is important because of the way in which it is conducted. These individual-level data measure the impact of candidate-to-voter communication, arguably the most important line of communication in a campaign. Herrnson and Patterson find that through strategies, including television advertising, candidates set the campaign agenda to bring their supporters in line. Their data indicate that candidates and voters agreed on the major issues of the election. The authors then show that this issue agreement can have an effect on vote choice. In most instances, voters who agreed with one of the candidates voted for that candidate. Other studies have attempted to examine the importance of campaign communications and messages, but they have relied on data that leave out explicit measures of the candidates' issue positions. Herrnson and Patterson succeed in making this crucial link.

The greatest pure methodological addition to the literature is found in chapter 6 by Iyengar and Petrocik. Given the review by Lau and Sigelman in chapter 2 that illustrates the strengths and weaknesses of both survey and experimental data, Iyengar and Petrocik employ both designs to answer these criticisms and to test their hypotheses. The consistent findings across the survey and experimental tests lend further credibility and reliability to their conclusions. Although their conclusions are not new—voters make their choice for president based on partisanship (the "partisan rule") and retrospective judgments of the current administration (the "basic rule")—through their methodological pluralism the authors reach the conclusion in a manner unlike any before them. Iyengar and Petrocik conclude that, although campaigns *do* activate the electorate, the net effect of this is close to nil. Since both sides in a presidential election receive a great deal of exposure, which translates into activation, the two sides in effect cancel each other out. Thus the election rests on partisanship and retrospective assessments of the current administration. However, the authors do not rule out that certain features of campaigns, such as get-out-the-vote efforts, *can* decide elections.

A quick reading of the chapters by Herrnson and Patterson and by Iyengar and Petrocik might lead one to believe that the two are at odds. In fact, they are complementary. Herrnson and Patterson show that campaign communication leads to issue agreement between candidates and voters and that this is likely due to partisanship. Iyengar and Petrocik reach a similar conclusion: campaign communications lead voters to employ either the party rule or the basic rule in making their choices. One difference in these two studies is the elective office that is under investigation. Herrnson and Patterson study elections for the U.S. House of Representatives, and Iyengar and Petrocik examine presidential contests. There are obvious fundamental differences between these types of races. For example, presidential elections are widely covered events, and many House elections are uncontested races that draw little attention even from local news outlets.

The authors also make novel normative judgments about political advertising and try to predict the future of television advertising in political campaigns. Nothing exhibits the fresh nature of these recommendations as does Jamieson, Waldman, and Sherr's *encouragement* of attack ads. This may sound outrageous given all the negative attention that negative ads have received in the popular press and in some academic circles. Negative ads have been demonized as a scourge in our electoral system, but that was under the traditional classification consisting of the false dichotomy between negative and positive. In light of Jamieson, Waldman, and Sherr's evidence that attack and contrast ads actually contain more policy information for public consumption, and Kahn and Kenney's findings that negative ads actually increase voters' knowledge of candidates and their positions, it seems that the more attack ads there are, the more informed voters will be.

However, we also agree with Kahn and Kenney's cautious view of negative advertising. Even though they argue that "negative advertisements may perform an important function in our electoral system" by providing information to the public, they may cross a dangerous line. Even though their evidence supports the hypothesis that negative advertisements inform the electorate, this should not give candidates or issue advocacy groups carte blanche to say anything about anyone. Clearly, creating a hard-hitting contrast ad that illustrates the issue positions of a candidate and his or her opponent is one thing. Distorting the record of a candidate, falsely attacking the character of a candidate, or purposely misleading voters is quite another. Jamieson, Waldman, and Sherr agree, arguing that attack (or contrast) ads must be accurate if they are to be encouraged as a positive part of democratic election campaigns. West also calls for interest group issue ads to be accurate and truthful if they are to improve democratic discourse.

The analyses by Jamieson, Waldman, and Sherr and by Kahn and Kenney tell us that negative ads contain more information than positive ads and that the electorate recalls this information more readily. What we do not know is how the electorate uses this information. Fortunately, we have evidence from Iyengar and Petrocik that even if some negative information is disseminated during a campaign, it is likely to reinforce a voter's partisan predisposition. Rather than manipulate, campaigns are found to enlighten. Iyengar and Petrocik dismiss the "hand wringing and condemnation of modern campaigns for their use of deceptive" messages, arguing instead that the electorate is more politically savvy than that. The electorate should be trusted to make the correct judgment on election day and should not be underestimated for their lack of political sophistication.

The chapters by Jamieson, Waldman, and Sherr, by Kahn and Kenney, and by Iyengar and Petrocik are all talking about one kind of advertisement—candidate-sponsored ads. West illustrates the need for reform in the area of issue advocacy. He offers three suggestions: do nothing, broaden disclosure, or regulate the content of issue ads.

Doing nothing may be analogous to the calls for infusing *more* money into the campaign system when many have called for finance reform and *less* money. Clearly this is unacceptable to West. A more plausible solution is also analogous to a proposed campaign finance reform—full and complete disclosure. This disclosure would occur on a number of fronts. Groups that advocate for a certain candidate (but get around the law by not employing the magic words "elect," "defeat," "vote for," or "vote against") must be held accountable by telling the viewing audience who they are while the ad is running on the screen (visual disclosure) and must be required to tell the public who is funding them (monetary disclosure). West also argues that a possible solution for the difficulties facing issue advocacy is enhanced regulation of those ads. "Ending the politics of personal destruction" became a cliché in 1999, but regulating the content of the issue ads run by an interest group (or any other group) likely will lead only to a court challenge. As West reports, "truth-in-communication codes" may be a solution on a state-by-state basis. The American Association of Political Consultants (AAPC), the professional organization for campaign consultants, itself has tried to encourage its members—the professionals who research, design, and produce many issue ad spots—to be more ethical in providing their services by encouraging them to sign the AAPC's own code of ethics. The jury is still out on the effectiveness of these measures.

Finally, this volume provides insights of a practical nature that are useful to students and practitioners of political advertising as we move into the next election cycle and beyond. The evidence provided by Jamieson, Waldman, and Sherr and and by Kahn and Kenney reinforces what political advertising practitioners already know—negative or attack advertising gets people's attention, and it works. The presence of this campaign tactic is not likely to disappear even though many have called for candidates to avoid using attack ads. Given other evidence in this volume, negative and attack ads may not be such a bad occurrence, as these types of ads contain policy information and inform the electorate that views them. In addition, these ads, among other campaign communications, activate individuals' partisan attachments in their vote choice, as shown by Iyengar and Petrocik.

In an effort to improve interest group issue advocacy campaigns, West challenges some of the actors involved to take responsibility for their actions. He calls for the media covering campaigns to do a better job of publicizing the unethical and stealthy campaigns of some issue advocates. He also calls on the issue advocacy groups to self-regulate and to look out for our representative democracy. To what extent should issue advocacy groups be unencumbered to say whatever they want however they want? Is the rise of issue advocacy helping or hindering our democratic way of life? Is the proliferation of issue advocacy groups adding to our pluralistic system, or is it contributing to hyperpluralism and a breakdown of the representative system?

Iyengar and Petrocik find that campaigns matter but that they have little net effect on the vote because competing campaigns cancel each other's effects. Television advertising, however, does help to lead voters to make their choice for president based on either the "party rule" or the "basic rule." Voters are "activated" by the campaign, its messages, and communications. What, then, is the net impact of the hundreds of millions of dollars spent on the 2000 campaign and beyond? Candidates such as Steve Forbes went on the air in mid-summer 1999; George W. Bush was all but anointed the Republican nominee; Vice President Al Gore and former senator Bill Bradley were battling in a primary-like atmosphere six months before a single voter cast a ballot in the Iowa caucuses or the New Hampshire primary; and the media devoted great amounts of print space and broadcast time to the 2000 presidential race in mid- to late-1999. However, Senator John McCain (R) focused his media campaign solely on New Hampshire and South Carolina in late 1999 to early 2000. This early advertising and media focus on campaign 2000 may mean that voters were being activated to move toward their partisan predispositions and retrospective evaluation of the Clinton administration in mid-1999.

The argument that campaigns and television advertising activate the electorate may cause us to pause even more given the likelihood that the role of issue advocacy groups will increase. As West illustrates, it is not likely that the part played by issue advocacy groups will diminish in future electoral cycles. Some groups were on the air as early as July and August 1999 talking about issues such as social security, taxes, medicare, term limits, gun control, and education. Although these ads did not mention candidates by name, voters could ascertain their targets. The activities of issue advocacy groups may mean that voters are being activated in this way too. If this is the case, and we will only know by testing this hypothesis systematically in future elections, we may be seeing the demise of the traditional campaign season—from Labor Day to election day. As Iyengar and Petrocik show, "Most of the vote in 1992 and 1996 was decided well before the onset of the fall campaign." With the television advertising and campaign activities of 1999 and early 2000, we can only hypothesize that activation had already begun and that, by the fall of 2000, the electorate already will have decided whom they want to be their next president. The impact of early and heavily televised political advertising will only be more pronounced in election cycles to come.

Reference

Ansolabehere, Stephen, and Shanto Iyengar. 1995. *Going Negative: How Political Advertisements Shrink and Polarize the Electorate*. Free Press.

Contributors

David A. Dulio is a research fellow at the Center for Congressional and Presidential Studies and a doctoral candidate in the Department of Government, School of Public Affairs, American University.

Paul S. Herrnson is a professor of government and politics at the University of Maryland, College Park.

Shanto Iyengar is a professor of communication and political science at Stanford University.

Kathleen Hall Jamieson is a professor of communication and dean of the Annenberg School for Communication at the University of Pennsylvania and director of the university's Annenberg Public Policy Center.

Kim Fridkin Kahn is an associate professor of political science at Arizona State University.

Patrick J. Kenney is an associate professor of political science at Arizona State University.

Richard R. Lau is a professor of political science at Rutgers University.

Candice J. Nelson is an associate professor of government and academic director of the Campaign Management Institute at American University. She is coeditor of *Campaigns and Elections, American Style* (with James A. Thurber).

Kelly D. Patterson is an associate professor in the Department of Political Science at Brigham Young University.

John R. Petrocik is a professor of political science and department chair at the University of Missouri.

Susan Sherr is a doctoral student at the Annenberg School for Communication and senior researcher on the Annenberg campaign discourse mapping project.

Lee Sigelman is a member of the Department of Political Science at George Washington University.

James A. Thurber is a professor of government at American University and director of the Center for Congressional and Presidential Studies and the center's institutes. He is the principal investigator for the Improving Campaign Conduct grant at American University, sponsored by the Pew Charitable Trusts.

Paul Waldman is a doctoral student at the Annenberg School for Communication and senior researcher on the Annenberg campaign discourse mapping project.

Darrell M. West is a professor of political science and director of the John Hazen White Sr. Public Opinion Laboratory at Brown University.

Index